Outdoor Gas Griddle

1500+ Days of Mouth-Watering and Simple Griddle Recipes to Become a Grill Master - Beginners and Advanced Users Friendly

CHARLES BURRELL

© **Copyright 2022 - All rights reserved.**

The content contained within this book may not be reproduced, duplicated or transmitted without direct written permission from the author or the publisher.

Under no circumstances will any blame or legal responsibility be held against the publisher, or author, for any damages, reparation, or monetary loss due to the information contained within this book. Either directly or indirectly.

Legal Notice:

This book is copyright protected. This book is only for personal use. You cannot amend, distribute, sell, use, quote or paraphrase any part, or the content within this book, without the consent of the author or publisher.

Disclaimer Notice:

Please note the information contained within this document is for educational and entertainment purposes only. All effort has been executed to present accurate, up to date, and reliable, complete information. No warranties of any kind are declared or implied. Readers acknowledge that the author is not engaging in the rendering of legal, financial, medical or professional advice. The content within this book has been derived from various sources. Please consult a licensed professional before attempting any techniques outlined in this book. By reading this document, the reader agrees that under no circumstances is the author responsible for any losses, direct or indirect, which are incurred as a result of the use of information contained within this document, including, but not limited to, — errors, omissions, or inaccuracies.

Table of Contents

Introduction 6
- Introduction to Outdoor Gas Griddle 6
- The Griddle Cooking Station: What Is It?.. 6
- The Main Features of the Outdoor Gas Griddle.. 6
- How to Use Your Griddle 7
- General Maintenance of Your Griddle 8
- How to Setup the Right Temperature 8
- The Essential Tools for Your Griddle 9
- How to Store Your Griddle 10
- What It Does 10

Breakfast Recipes 11
- Breakfast Hash Recipe 11
- **Buttermilk Pancakes** 12
- **Oatmeal Pancakes** 13
- Camping Griddle Breakfast 13
- **Blackstone Monte Cristo** 14
- **Broccoli Pancakes** 15
- **Tomato Scrambled Egg** 16
- Chocolate Pancake 16
- Cauliflower Patties 17
- **Cheesy Ham and Pineapple Sandwich** 18
- **Croque Madame** 18
- **Johnny Cakes with Bourbon Salted Caramel Sauce** 19
- **Italian Breakfast Lavash** 20
- **French Toast** 21
- **Kale Omelet** 21
- **Breakfast Sandwich with Bacon and Cheese** 22
- **Turkey Pesto Panini** 23
- **Cauliflower Hash Browns** 23
- **Spinach Pancakes** 24

Burgers Recipes 25
- **Lamb and Cucumber Burger** 25
- Marinated Portobello Cheese Burgers 25
- **Croque Ham Cheese Burgers** 26
- **Beef and Corn Burgers** 27
- **Bulgur Beet Burgers** 28
- Marinated Portobello Cheese Burgers 28
- **Garlic Parsley Cheese Sandwiches** 29
- **Turkey Burger Patty Melts** 30
- **Garlicky Pork Burgers** 30
- **Cheese and Tomato Burgers** 31

Vegetables and Side Dishes Recipes 33
- **Italian Zucchini Slices** 33
- **Vegetable Skewers** 33
- **Vegetable Yakisoba** 34
- **Grilled Vegetables** 35
- **Fried Rice on the Griddle** 36
- **Lemon Garlic Artichokes** 36
- **Blistered Green Beans** 37
- Steamed Carrots in Ranch Dressing 37
- Zucchini Squash Mix 38
- Sautéed Savoury Green Beans 39
- **Easy Seared Green Beans** 39
- **Grilled Hash Browns** 40
- **Crispy Cooked Potatoes** 41
- **Parmesan Zucchini** 41
- **Fried Green Tomatoes with Parsley** 42
- **Tasty Cornish Game Hen** 43

Poultry Recipes 44
- **California Seared Chicken** 44
- Chili Lime Chicken with Sesame Seed 44
- Seared Spicy Boneless Chicken Thighs 45

- Honey Balsamic Marinated Chicken 46
- Glazed Chicken Wings 47
- Herb Roasted Turkey in Chicken Broth 47
- Butterflied Chicken 48
- Lemony Chicken Breast 49
- Sweet and Spicy Chicken Breast 50
- Marinated Chicken Breast 51
- Chicken Wings with Sweet Red Chili and Peach Glaze 51
- Chicken Phillies 52
- Teriyaki Chicken Stir Fry 53
- Chicken Teriyaki 54
- Sizzling Chicken Fajitas 54
- Hawaiian Chicken Skewers 55
- Fiery Italian Chicken Skewers 56
- Chicken Thighs with Ginger-Sesame Glaze 57
- Buffalo Chicken Wings 58

Turkey Recipes 59
- Cured Turkey Drumstick 59
- Bourbon Turkey 60
- Brine-Marinated Turkey Breast 61
- Smoked Turkey Tabasco 62
- Jalapeno Turkey in Broth 63
- Mayo Turkey 64

Pork Recipes 66
- Herb-rusted Mediterranean Pork Tenderloin 66
- Paprika Dijon Pork Tenderloin 66
- Pork Ribs with Low-Sugar Ketchup 67
- Pork Chops with Pineapple and Bacon 68
- Baked Egg and Bacon-Stuffed Peppers 69
- Sausage Mixed Grill 69
- Cuban Pork Chops 70
- Spicy Cajun Pork Chops 70
- Teriyaki-Marinated Pork Sirloin Tip Roast 71
- Prime Rib of Pork 71
- Tender Griddle Loin Chops 72
- Florentine Ribeye Pork Loin 72

Beef Recipes 74
- Grilled Flat Iron 74
- Sweet e Spicy Teriyaki Beef Kebabs 74
- Herb-Marinated Steak Tips 74
- Butte Montana- Style Beef Pasty 75
- Sear Ribeye with Smoked Garlic e Vegetables 76
- Seared Garlic Ribeye with Carrots, Asparagus e Gremolata 77
- Garlicky Sirloin Beef with Parmesan 77
- Juicy NY Strip Steak Griddle 78

Lamb Recipes 79
- Grilled Lamb Burgers 79
- Lamb Shank 79
- Lamb Skewers 80
- Lamb Ribs Rack 81
- Lamb Chops 81
- Cocoa Crusted Grilled Flank Steak .. 81
- Bone In-Turkey Breast 82
- Grilled Lamb Sandwiches 83
- Yan's Grilled Quarters 83

Fish and Seafood Recipes 85
- Grilled King Crab Legs 85
- Cajun Smoked Catfish 85
- Grilled Tilapia 86
- Salmon with Togarashi 87
- Crab stuffed Lingcod 87
- Smoked Shrimp 89

Salmon Fillets with Basil Butter e Broccolini 89
Spiced Snapper with Mango and Red Onion Salad 90
Spiced Salmon 91
Glazed Salmon 91
Sweet e Sour Salmon 92
Cod Parcel 93
Spiced Whole Trout 93
Simple Haddock 94
Tuna Skewers 94
Crusted Scallops 95
Shrimp Kabobs 95

Appetizer Recipes 97
Scallops Orange Skewers 97
Tasty Bread Pizza 97
Corn Cakes 98
Tuna Patties 98
Quick Cheese Toast 99
Tomato Avocado Bruschetta 99
Spicy Chicken Burger Patties 100
Walnuts Bowls 100
Radish with Herb Cheese 101
Healthy Broccoli 101
Easy Pineapple Slices 102
Tortilla Pizza 102
Chickpea Burger Patties 103
Veggie Patties 103

Dessert Recipes 105
Honey Fruit on the Griddle 105
Yummy Apple Pie on the Griddle with Cinnamon 105
Simple Coconut 105
Vanilla Bacon Chocolate Chip Cookies 106
Walnut Chocolate Chip Cookies 107
Cinnamon Apple Cobbler 107
Bananas in Caramel Sauce 108
Ice Cream Bread with Chocolate Chips 108
Sugar Pumpkin Seeds with Cinnamon 109
Mint Julep Peaches 109
Watermelon with yogurt 110
Pound Cake with Sour Cherry Syrup 111
Seasonal Fruit with Gelato 111
Griddled Strawberry e Pineapple 112
French Toast Skewers 112
Cream Cheese e Jam Stuffed 113
Chocolate-Stuffed French Toast 113
Chocolate Cherry Griddled 114
Chocolate Marshmallow Waffle 114
Chocolate S'mores 115
Cinnamon Roll Pancakes 115
Vanilla Cupcakes 116
Griddle Fruit with Cream 117
Apple Pie on the Griddle 118
Griddle Layered Cake 118

Conclusions 120
Additional Features 120
Energy Efficiency/Environmental Impact 120

Introduction

Introduction to Outdoor Gas Griddle

It might be quite difficult to prepare food for various outdoor activities. This is due to the fact that when you are away from home and outdoors, you sometimes lack all of the culinary equipment and tools that you require. Multiple-burner gas stoves that allow you to prepare a range of things are a blessing. All of those needs are satisfied by an outdoor gas griddle without sacrificing quality. It is constructed of premium stainless steel. You can prepare meals more easily, regardless of your degree of competence, thanks to thick, hot-rolled steel that stores and distributes heat energy. If you want to organize a large outside BBQ, an outdoor gas griddle is one of those things you absolutely must have.

The Griddle Cooking Station: What Is It?

The Griddle is an outdoor cooking appliance that uses gas and has a flat top surface to distribute heat steadily and evenly. It can cook anything that is cooked in a frying pan, including eggs, French toast, home fries, stir-fries, sausages, and bacon. While amateur BBQers frequently utilize the Griddle, professional cooks may also use it. Heavy, cold-rolled steel that doesn't stick, dent, bruise, or corrode makes up the flat top surface of the object. The griddle's legs can be folded, making it simple to move it from one place to another. Generally speaking, griddles make cooking easy, fast, and effective.

The Main Features of the Outdoor Gas Griddle

Are you familiar with the fundamental specs of the outdoor gas griddle?

For your breakfast, lunch, and supper, it features a flat surface that absorbs the juice from a portion of food. They are cooked with a crispy crust, a soft core, and a rich taste, from toast to steak!

Check out all the features to learn more about the fundamentals and advantages of using an outdoor gas griddle. It's a simple and enjoyable method to cook outside. Here are the top 6 requirements for outdoor gas griddles.

The Griddle with the Flat Top

This is where all the action takes place! You prepare meals in this area. Using the proper implements, you may lay a piece of raw beef on the griddle. In only a few minutes, your meal is cooked. The cooktop is made of cold-rolled steel and is sleek and black. This indicates that nothing is damaged—not even wrinkles, tears, rips, or holes. There are no chilly patches since cooking is distributed uniformly throughout the whole surface. The hamburger is guaranteed to be cooked equally throughout, and the center will taste just as excellent.

The Grease Collector

All of the meat's liquid is trapped in with the meal due to the flat lid. All of the remaining dripping is collected by the grease collector. This is good news if you detest cleaning up after cooking. It's quite simple to clear this grease trap. Mix water and soap to carefully wipe away the oil. That's all there is to it.

The Burners

To switch on, start a fire, and start cooking, all you have to do is pull the trigger.

Turn on the propane by pressing the ignition button. A black stone gas griddle has various heating zones since it has many burners. At the same time, there are low, medium, medium-high, high, and all of these temperatures.

The outdoor gas griddle's heat control is simple to use. You can't control the charcoal fire while using a charcoal barbecue, which results in overcooking. It is operated with the touch of your fingertips in an outdoor gas griddle. It enables you to precisely choose the preferred heat.

Portable Machine

The gas grill outside is transportable. This grill's components may all be transported anywhere with ease. From dawn to dusk, cook the cuisine of your choosing wherever you go.

How to Use Your Griddle

1. Never season food with animal fat first. A thin film of oil is left on your griddle after each seasoning. Bacon and other animal fats include salts that stick to your griddle after usage and damage it. Therefore, avoid seasoning your griddle with bacon fat at first.

2. Use a microfiber cloth to apply oil-based seasoning to the cooking surface of a gas grill. To season your griddle, you can use a variety of oils. Coconut oil, canola oil, grapeseed oil, maize oil, and vegetable oil are some of the greatest oils that may be utilized. Verify that the oil you're using hasn't been refined or filtered.

3. Set the griddle to its highest heat setting. All burners should be turned on. After 10 to 15 minutes, add the oil.

4. Drizzle the griddle with 2 to 3 teaspoons of oil. Use a cotton cloth to apply oil to the griddle's whole surface, including the vertical edges. Use a dishtowel that has been folded over on itself multiple times. Avoid getting burned during this operation. Avoid touching the hot oil with your fingertips.

5. Hold off until the griddle stops smoking, which should be 10 minutes. Five or six times in total, repeat the preceding action.

6. Carry out the steps once more after using the griddle. Using this technique, you produce several oil layers that will preserve your griddle.

General Maintenance of Your Griddle

Your griddle needs to be cleaned while it is still heated.

Don't wait too long or the leftover food may dry out and become difficult to remove. Put some water on the griddle and, if required, adjust the heat so that steam is produced from the water. Start removing the food scraps using an iron kitchen spatula. Once all the crumbs have been removed, turn off the heat and thoroughly dry the griddle with some absorbent paper or a kitchen towel.

The griddle is then covered with 3 spoons of oil, which you spread with a dish towel. You may now save your griddle until you need it again.

Keep in mind that the griddle only has to be smooth; it need not be flawless.

How to Setup the Right Temperature

Griddling has several benefits over other cooking techniques. More food is in direct contact with the heat source, which causes browning to happen more quickly. This browning, which adds a delectable crust and enticing scents, results in a more savory meal. The first step in obtaining the correct level of browning is applying the proper quantity of heat.

However, caramelization (the deactivation of proteins) and taste development do not start until temperatures reach between 320 and 400 degrees Fahrenheit (160 and 204 degrees Celsius) and 356 to 370 degrees Fahrenheit, respectively. Browning starts around 310°F (154°C) (180-188 degrees Celsius).

This chemical procedure is known as the Maillard Process. When exposed to extremely high temperatures, proteins and carbohydrates are broken down (denature). The most visible signs of denaturation are changes in colors, tastes, and scents.

When the griddle's temperature is set too low (between 300°F and 320°F), food must be exposed to heat for a longer amount of time in order to cause this chemical reaction.

Some people consider a piece of red meat to be perfectly cooked when the outside crust achieves a temperature of at least 310 °F(155°C). This indicates that the beef's outside temperature has above 310°F, and an accurate digital thermometer will validate the inside temperature.
Use a griddle heated to 350-
375 degrees Fahrenheit to achieve the optimum caramelization and interior doneness. You may keep an eye on the griddle's surface temperature and identify hot and cold spots.
Avoid these regions as much as you can to prevent uneven cooking and to maintain a constant level of food quality.
To obtain the greatest taste from your cuisine, use these temperature guidelines the next time you heat up the griddle.

The Essential Tools for Your Griddle

Before you can start grilling, you will need extra supplies and accessories. You will also want a few more crucial cooking tools in addition to the griddle itself. Tongs, spatulas, and basting brushes are essential tools for grilling.

Furthermore, you must purchase at least two sets of tongs, one for moving the coals and the other for turning the food while it cooks. To assess whether the meat and poultry you are cooking are done, you may also buy a meat thermometer.

To avoid flare-ups and collect drips, it is also advised to incorporate a drip pan made of metal foil. 1.5 inches is the ideal pan depth. Some chefs make a delicious sauce or gravy using the drippings. Plastic spray bottles filled with water are helpful for putting out flare-ups while using charcoal grills.

Water is not advised for use with gas grills, though. Hinged wire baskets are necessary if you plan to prepare fish and veggies. These wire baskets have been created especially for vegetables and seafood that can break when turned with a spatula. Metal or bamboo skewers are ideal for kebabs.

Cooking Pans

When you hear the word "griddle pan," what comes to mind? A lovely stack of pancakes or French toast would come to mind. Maybe barbecued chicken or big, juicy hamburgers come to mind. You are aware that a top-notch griddle pan may be utilized to make a broad range of delicious dishes, either way. You should have a variety of pots, pans, and other cooking utensils if you cook frequently. Make sure you have the necessary tools, such as a coffee maker, microwave, blender, etc. The right tools must be available as well. The quality of the meal would degrade if you only buy cheap kitchen equipment and gadgets. Both the quality of your meal and the durability of your kitchenware will suffer. Various foods may be prepared in the griddle pan. For instance, you could make fried potatoes, French toast, prairie chicken, hamburgers, meat that has been seared, etc. A griddle pan is a need that is frequently used in the kitchen. It's crucial to keep a few things in mind while looking for a griddle pan. Put quality first. A pan that will last for many years is what you want, not one that will crack or appear worn out after only a few years. Find something of excellent quality at a fair price. Some high-end brands are occasionally of mediocre quality. Read reviews to identify places where you can get both quality and a fair price.When you own a griddle, you should become familiar with how to use and maintain it.

How to Store Your Griddle

You must preserve your outdoor gas griddle carefully if you don't want it to rust within a few weeks after you get it.

You might only use them on the weekends when the whole family gets together, typically on Sundays when everyone can be there and you can rekindle your relationship. You might do it once a week or once a month—perhaps during get-togethers with your former coworkers and/or buddies.

Whatever your situation, it's crucial to keep your griddle in top condition for the next occasion, which necessitates storing it in the ideal location throughout the intervals between cookouts. You should constantly make sure that your gas griddle is kept in the ideal location in your house.

And where is the ideal location? A dry, cool location. You must keep your griddle in a constantly dry environment. Avoid wet areas if you want to preserve your griddle in good condition and prevent rust at all costs.

Make sure the environment is not extremely warm as well. The propane tank in your griddle may not be safe in hot settings; consider a fire. So, always maintain them at a comfortable temperature. If you're storing your griddle in a closet, keep everything away from it. Make certain they have plenty of room to breathe. Additionally, if you choose to keep them in your garage, be sure to regularly check on them to clean and dust them.In order to shield your griddle from any harm, corrosion, scratches, and dust, you need also get a heavy-duty canvas cover. Even after years of usage, keeps them in brand-new condition.

What It Does

The Griddle functions in a manner that is comparable to how a regular griddle is used for cooking. In both cases, a flat surface is heated, and this heats the food being cooked. The Griddle, however, features temperature control valves, so there is no need to remove the cooking surface from direct heat. Propane or butane LPG bottle gas is used by the Griddle as a fuel source to start controlled fires. The built-in igniter needles light a fire in the burner tube when the Griddle is turned on and heated to a specific temperature using the control valves.

The griddle top is heated to the required temperature by the burner tube, which is located beneath the griddle top.

Food is cooked right on the hot Griddle Top, as opposed to the usual Griddle. The Griddle's ability to fry, grill, and sear are due to the heat produced. Here are the detailed instructions for lighting the Griddle: 1. Verify that the ignition switch's battery is placed properly.

2. Open the control valve at the gas cylinder and on the gas bottle to let the gas out.

3. Rotate the Griddle's control valves until the indication line is pointing upward.

4. Quickly depress the ignition switch. Before cooking every meal, there should be a click, and the Griddle should be preheated for 3–5 minutes.

Breakfast Recipes

Breakfast Hash Recipe

(**Preparation time**: 10 min | **Cook time**: 30 min | **Servings**: 10)

Ingredients:

- 2 Bags Frozen Potatoes O'Brien
- 1 Sausage Rope
- 8 Slices Thick Cut Bacon
- 12 Eggs
- 1/2 Red Onion
- Green Onion

Instructions:

- Start your griddle and oiled it.
- After your griddle has been warmed and oiled, turn the heat all the way down.
- Make sure you have two spatulas and a scraper on hand to prepare this dinner.
- Spread the frozen potatoes out onto your griddle first, so they can begin to defrost and brown.
- whisk (In a large mixing bowl) together the scrambled eggs. To make the eggs fluffier, I add roughly 1/2 cup of water to them.
- Cut up your sausage, onion, and bacon while the potatoes are cooking.
- Push the potatoes to the other side of the griddle, and at this point, I added my onions to the potatoes on the griddle.
- Place the bacon on the griddle's other side and increase the heat on that burner so it cooks faster.
- Place the sausage and cook over low heat; it will cook quickly enough at this temperature.
- Allow them to cook until the bacon has reveryed the desired crispiness.
- Pour the egg mixture on the opposite side of the griddle after moving the meat into the potato mixture.
- The eggs will scramble quickly, so I stir them about with one of the spatulas to ensure that they do.
- Start mixing your eggs into your potatoes and meat combination when they're almost done.
- When they're thoroughly mixd, sprinkle with cheese and turn the griddle off.
- While the cheese was melting, I dashed in and made toast.
- Serve and have fun!!

Buttermilk Pancakes

(**Preparation time:** 15 minutes | **Cooking time:** 5 minutes | **Servings:** 12)

Per serving: Calories 146, Total Fat 5 g, Saturated Fat 2.8 g, Cholesterol 42 mg, Sodium 211 mg, Total Carbs 21.9 g, Fiber 0.4 g, Sugar 9.1 g, Protein 3.4 g

Ingredients:

- 2 tablespoons of blackened seasoning
- 1 lb. of chicken breasts
- 2 tablespoons of butter, melted

Instructions:

- 1½ cups all-purpose flour
- 2 tablespoons sugar
- 1 teaspoon baking powder

- ½ teaspoon baking soda
- ½ teaspoon salt
- 2 large eggs
- 1 cup buttermilk
- ¼ cup unsalted butter, melted
- 1 teaspoon vanilla extract
- 6 tablespoons maple syrup

Oatmeal Pancakes

(**Preparation time:** 15 minutes | **Cooking time:** 5 minutes | **Servings:** 8)

Per serving: Calories 148, Total Fat 5.7 g, Saturated Fat 1.5 g, Cholesterol 23 mg Sodium 170 mg, Total Carbs 21.5 g, Fiber 1.6 g, Sugar 10.2 g, Protein 3.8 g

Ingredients:

- ¾ cup old-fashioned oats
- ¾ cup oat flour
- 1 teaspoon baking powder
- ½ teaspoon salt
- 1 egg
- 1 cup milk
- 2 tablespoons vegetable oil
- 4 tablespoons honey

Instructions:

- Preheat the Outdoor Gas Griddle to medium heat.
- Mix together the oats, oat flour, brown sugar, baking powder, baking soda, spices and salt in a bowl.
- In a second bowl, add egg, milk, and oil and beat until well combined.
- In the bowl of egg mixture, add the flour mixture and mix until just moistened.
- Grease the griddle lightly.
- Place about ¼ cup of the mixture onto the griddle and spread in an even layer.
- Repeat with the remaining mixture.
- Cook each pancake for about 2-3 minutes or until golden brown.
- Flip the pancakes and cook for 1-2 minutes or until golden brown.
- Serve warm with the drizzling of honey.

Camping Griddle Breakfast

(**Preparation time**: 10 min | **Cook time**: 25 min | **Servings**: 5)

Ingredients:

- Eggs
- 4 Pounds Gold Potatoes
- 1 Pound Bacon
- 5 Polish sausages
- Cheese
- Minced Garlic
- Salt
- Pepper

Instructions:

- Your potatoes should be washed and dried.
- All of the vegetables should be sliced and diced, and the sausages should be polished.
- When you heat up your griddle, brush it with a little oil or bacon fat to aid in nonsticking and sauteing the food.
- Mix the potatoes, onion, and polish sausage on your griddle.
- Add salt and pepper as needed.
- Cook until potatoes are fork-tender.
- Remove the potatoes and keep warm on a dish.
- Fry your bacon till it's done to your liking, and then fry your eggs at the same time (or scrambled eggs)
- Serve everything at the same time and have fun!! We used shredded cheese as a topping, but you could also use sour cream!

Blackstone Monte Cristo

(**Preparation time:** 15 minutes | **Cooking time:** 10 minutes | **Servings:** 6)

Ingredients:

- 4 eggs
- 1/3 cup of half and half
- 12 pieces of white bread
- 2 tbsp mayo
- 2 tbsp mustard
- 18 thin slices of swiss or gruyere cheese
- 2 pounds deli thin-sliced ham
- powdered sugar
- raspberry jam

Instructions:

- Preheat your griddle in a low heat setting.
- In a large shallow bowl, whisk together the eggs and half and half until well blended.
- One side of your bread should be drenched in egg wax. Place in a single layer on a parchment-lined baking sheet, eggy side down.
- 1 tsp mayo and 1 tsp mustard on every sandwich bread pair, mayo on one and mustard on the other.
- On every slice of bread, place one piece of cheese. Distribute the ham evenly across the 12 slices of bread.
- Place one half of every sandwich bread pair with the remaining 6
- pieces of cheese. (Every sandwich should include three slices of cheese.)
- To make whole sandwiches, join the sandwich pieces together.
- Butter the griddle well and arrange the sandwiches on it. Cover with a big spatula and gently press down.
- Cook the egg mixture is set and the bread is toasted, then flip and brown the other side.
- Remove from the oven, sprinkle with powdered sugar, and serve with raspberry jam on the side.

Broccoli Pancakes

(**Preparation time:** 15 minutes | **Cooking time:** 10 minutes | **Servings:** 5)

Per serving: Calories 167, Total Fat 2.5 g, Saturated Fat 1 g, Cholesterol 44 mg, Sodium 77 mg, Total Carbs 29.5 g, Fiber 1.9 g, Sugar 2.9 g, Protein 6.6 g

Ingredients:

- 1 cup broccoli florets
- 1 small onion, chopped roughly
- 1 garlic clove, peeled
- 1 egg
- ½ cup whole milk
- 1 cup all-purpose flour
- 1 teaspoon baking powder
- 5 fresh chives, chopped
- 1 tablespoon fresh chervil, chopped
- Salt and ground black pepper, to taste

Instructions:

- Preheat the Outdoor Gas Griddle to medium-high heat.

- Add the broccoli, onion and garlic into a blender and pulse until finely chopped.
- Add the egg, milk, flour and baking powder and pulse on medium speed until a thick mixture forms.
- Transfer the broccoli mixture into a bowl.
- Add the chives, chervil, salt and black pepper and stir to combine.
- Grease the griddle lightly.
- Place about 2 tablespoons of the mixture onto the griddle and spread in an even layer.
- Repeat with the remaining mixture.
- Cook the pancakes for about 3 minutes.
- Carefully twist the pancakes and keep cooking for about 2 minutes or until golden brown.
- Serve warm.

Tomato Scrambled Egg

(**Preparation time:** 5 minutes | **Cooking time:** 10 minutes | **Servings:** 2)

Per serving: Calories 266, Total fat 14g, Protein 33g, Carbs 2g

Ingredients:

- 1 tablespoon of olive oil
- 2 eggs, lightly beaten
- Salt and pepper to taste
- 2 tablespoons of fresh basil, chopped
- 1/2 tomato, chopped

Instructions:

- Preheat your griddle at medium-high temperature.
- Apply oil to the griddle's surface.
- Cook till the tomatoes have softened.
- Combine together the eggs, basil, pepper, & salt.
- Cook till the eggs are set on top of the tomatoes by pouring the egg mixture over them. Enjoy your meal.

Chocolate Pancake

(**Preparation Time:** 10 minutes | **Cooking Time:** 10 minutes| **Servings:** 4)

Per serving: Calories 138, Fat 12 g, Carbohydrates 11 g, Sugar 8 g, Protein 4.5 g, Cholesterol 82 mg

Ingredients:

- 2 eggs
- 1/2 tsp baking powder
- 2 tbsp erythritol
- 1 1/2 tbsp cocoa powder
- 1/4 cup ground flaxseed
- 2 tbsp water
- 1 tsp nutmeg
- 1 tsp cinnamon
- 1/4 tsp salt

Istructions:

- In a bowl, mix ground flaxseed, baking powder, erythritol, cocoa powder, spices, and salt.
- Add eggs and stir well.
- Add water and stir until batter is well combined.
- Preheat the griddle to medium-low heat.
- Spray griddle top with cooking spray.
- Pour a large spoonful of batter on a hot griddle top and make a pancake.
- Cook pancake for 3–4 minutes on each side.
- Serve and enjoy.

Cauliflower Patties

(**Preparation time**: 15 minutes | **Cook time**: 15 minutes | **Serves**: 6)

Per Serving: Calories 155 Fat 10 g, Carbs 11.1 g, Sugar 3.9 g, Protein 8.1 , Cholesterol 60 mg

Ingredients:

- 2 eggs
- 1 large head cauliflower, cut into florets
- 1 tablespoon butter
- ½ teaspoon turmeric
- 1 tablespoon nutrition yeast
- ⅔ cup almond flour
- ¼ teaspoon black pepper
- ½ teaspoon salt

Instructions:

- Grease the cooking surface of the griddle with butter.
- Turn on the 4 burners and turn their knobs to medium heat.
- Let the Griddle preheat for 5 minutes.
- Add cauliflower florets to a suitable pot.
- Pour enough water to cover the cauliflower florets. Bring to boil for 8-10
- minutes.
- Drain cauliflower well and transfer in food processor and process until it looks like rice.
- Transfer cauliflower rice into the suitable bowl.
- Add the rest of the recipe's ingredients except for butter to the bowl and stir to combine.
- Make small patties from cauliflower mixture and place on preheated griddle top.
- Cook for almost 3-4 minutes on each side or until lightly golden brown.
- Serve.

Cheesy Ham and Pineapple Sandwich

(**Preparation time:** 10 minutes | **Cooking time:** 20 minutes | **Servings:** 4)

Per serving: Calories: 594; Sodium: 3184 mg; Dietary Fiber: 0.3 g; Fat: 40.3 g; Carbs: 4.7 g; Protein: 47.7 g

Ingredients:

- (10 ounces) package deli sliced ham
- Pineapple rings
- Slices Swiss cheese
- 8 slices of thick bread
- Butter, softened, for brushing

Instructions:

- Butter the bread and heat your griddle to medium heat.
- On top of each piece of bread, stack 1/4 of the ham, a pineapple ring, and 1 slice of cheese.
- Griddle the sandwiches.

Croque Madame

(**Preparation time:** 10 minutes | **Cooking time:** 10 minutes | **Servings:** 4)

Per serving: Calories: 538; Sodium: 1019 mg; Dietary Fiber: 2.4 g; Fat: 35.2 g; Carbs: 17.8 g; Protein: 36.9 g

Ingredients:

- 1 tbsp butter
- 1 tbsp flour
- 2/3 cup milk
- 4 slices thick-cut bread
- 3 slices black forest ham
- 3 slices gruyere cheese
- Salt and black pepper
- 2 eggs

Instructions:

- Add the milk after whisking just until browned. Stir the sauce until it becomes thick. Season after removing from the fire.
- Your griddle should be heated to medium. Each piece of bread is brushed with butter on one side and generously topped with bechamel sauce on the other.
- Top each sandwich with two slices of ham. Place there and cook till golden brown on the griddle. Place the gruyere cheese
- on top after flipping the sandwiches.
- Cook and serve.

Johnny Cakes with Bourbon Salted Caramel Sauce

(**Preparation time:** 10 minutes | **Cooking time:** 25 minutes | **Servings:** 4)

Ingredients:

- 1 cup All-purpose Glour
- 1 cup coarse Cornmeal
- 1 tablespoon Baking Powder
- 2 tablespoons Sugar
- 3 large Eggs
- ¼ cup liquid Bacon fat
- 1 cup Buttermilk
- Bourbon Salted Caramel Sauce:
- ½ cup Bourbon
- ¼ cup Water
- 1 cup granulated Sugar

- 3 tablespoon Unsalted Butter
- 1 cup Heavy Cream
- 1 teaspoon Vanilla Extract
- 2 teaspoons kosher Salt

Instructions:

- Combine the bourbon, water, and sugar in a large sauté pan. Bring to a low simmer over medium-high heat, stirring occasionally, until the bubbles become huge and the color turns a faint amber. Mix until it is completely melted and integrated. Combine the heavy cream, vanilla extract, and salt in a mixing bowl.
- Mix cornmeal, baking powder and flour.
- Add the eggs and bacon fat to a separate mixing dish and whisk well.
- In the flour and cornmeal basin, crack the eggs and add the bacon fat. 12 cup buttermilk, mixed evenly with a spatula To achieve the desired consistency, add more buttermilk.

Italian Breakfast Lavash

(**Preparation time:** 5 minutes | **Cooking time:** 15 minutes | **Servings:** 4)

Per serving: Calories 266, Total fat 14g, Protein 33g, Carbs 2g

Ingredients:

- 2 Lavash Flat Breads
- ½ lb Prosciutto, deli sliced
- ½ lb Capicola, deli sliced
- ½ lb Genoa Salami, deli sliced thin
- ½ lb Mortadella, deli sliced
- ½ lb Mozzarella, deli sliced
- ½ lb Provolone cheese, deli sliced thin
- 4 Eggs
- Balsamic Glaze
- Cento, hot pepper spread
- 2 c Arugula
- 1 tbsp Extra Virgin Olive Oil
- Salt & Pepper, to taste
- Spray extra light tasting olive oil

Instructions:

- Preheat the griddle to a low temperature.

- Prepare the arugula with extra-virgin olive oil and season with salt and pepper.
- Spray one side of the lavash bread lightly with oil and lay it on the griddle.
- On the griddle, cook 2 eggs per lavash to desired doneness while adding provolone cheese, Italian meats, and provolone cheese on top. Place the cheese against the lavash to act as a glue to keep the sandwich together. Spread some spicy pepper spread on top.
- Remove the cooked eggs from the griddle and place them evenly on one side of the lavash.
- To each sandwich, add about a cup of arugula. Drizzle balsamic glaze over the top. To make a sandwich, fold the lavash in half.
- Enjoy by cutting it in half or thirds.

French Toast

(**Preparation time:** 15 minutes | **Cooking time:** 6 minutes | **Servings:** 4)

Per serving: Calories 198, Total Fat 6.4 g, Saturated Fat 1.6 g, Cholesterol 165 mg, Sodium 268 mg, Total Carbs 28.2 g, Fiber 5.5 g, Sugar 9.6 g, Protein 11 g

Ingredients:

- ¼ cup milk
- 4 eggs
- 2 tablespoons sugar
- ½ teaspoon vanilla extract
- 1 teaspoon ground cinnamon
- ¼ teaspoon ground nutmeg
- 8 thick-cut bread slices
- ½ cup fresh strawberries, hulled and sliced

Instructions:

- Preheat the Outdoor Gas Griddle to low heat.
- In a shallow baking dish, add milk, eggs, sugar, vanilla extract, cinnamon, and nutmeg and beat until well combined.
- Dip each bread slice in milk mixture for about 5-10 seconds per side.
- Grease the griddle generously.
- Place the slices onto the griddle and cook for about 3 minutes per side.
- Serve with the topping of strawberry slices.

Kale Omelet

(**Preparation time:** 5 minutes | **Cooking time:** 10 minutes | **Servings:** 3)

Ingredients:

- 1 tablespoon of fresh sage, chopped
- 4 eggs
- 1/2 teaspoon of pepper
- 4 cups of kale, chopped
- 1/2 teaspoon of salt
- 1/3 cup of parmesan cheese, grated

Instructions:

- 1.Preheat your griddle to medium-high temperature.
- 2.Coat the top of the griddle using cooking spray.
- 3.Cook for a few minutes, or till kale has wilted, on a heated griddle top. In a mixing vessel, whisk together the eggs, then add the parmesan, sage, pepper,
- & salt.
- 4.Pour the egg mixture over kale, cook for around 8-10 minutes, or till the egg mixture is stiff. Enjoy your servings.

Breakfast Sandwich with Bacon and Cheese

(**Preparation time:** 10 minutes | **Cooking time:** 10 minutes | **Servings:** 4)

Per serving: Calories 470, Total fat 21g, Protein 38g, Carbs 10g

Ingredients:

- 4 tablespoons of Swiss grated cheese
- 4 round rolls sandwiches
- 4 tablespoons of ketchup
- 2 slices of bacon
- Salt and pepper to taste

Instructions:

- Begin by removing the tops of the sandwiches, remove the inside section of the sandwiches with a spoon, being careful not to damage or crack the crust.
- Fill each sandwich using a small amount of ketchup, place the bacon on top of the tomato, cut it into little pieces. Preheat your Griddle at 400°F for direct cooking in the meanwhile. Brush an oven-safe baking pan using olive oil.
- Arrange the sandwiches inside the pan, spacing them out as much as possible, complete salt, pepper, and grated Swiss cheese.
- Put the pan onto the griddle and cook for around 15 minutes, remove as soon as it's done and serve right away.

Turkey Pesto Panini

(**Preparation time:** 5 minutes | **Cooking time:** 6 minutes | **Servings:** 2)

Per serving: Calories 266, Total fat 14g, Protein 33g, Carbs 2g

Ingredients:

- 1 tbsp olive oil
- 3 slices French bread
- 1/2 cup pesto sauce
- 4 slices mozzarella cheese
- 2 cups chopped leftover turkey
- 1 Roma tomato, thinly sliced
- 1 avocado, halved, seeded, peeled, and sliced

Instructions:

- Preheat griddle to medium-high heat.
- Place 2 slices with the olive oil side down on the griddle.
- Spread 2 tbsp pesto over 1 side of French bread.
- Top with one slice of mozzarella, turkey, tomatoes, avocado, a second slice of mozzarella, and top with the second half of bread to make a sandwich; repeat with remaining slices of bread.
- Cook about 2–3
- minutes per side.
- Serve warm with your favorite salad or soup.

Cauliflower Hash Browns

(**Preparation time:** 10 minutes | **Cooking time:** 10 minutes | **Servings:** 6)

Per serving: Calories: 80; Fat: 5 g; Carbohydrates: 3 g; Sugar: 1 g; Protein: 5 g; Cholesterol: 46 mg

Ingredients:

- 1 egg
- 3 cups cauliflower, grated
- 3/4 cup cheddar cheese, shredded
- 1/8 tsp pepper
- 1/4 tsp garlic powder
- 1/4 tsp cayenne pepper
- 1/2 tsp salt

Instructions:

- Preheat the griddle to medium-low heat.
- Put all the ingredients into the bowl and mix well.
- Spray griddle top with cooking spray.
- Make 6 hash browns from mixture and place on hot griddle top and cook until golden brown from both sides.
- Serve and enjoy.

Spinach Pancakes

(**Preparation time:** 10 minutes | **Cooking time:** 10 minutes | **Servings:** 6)

Per serving: Calories 266, Total fat 14g, Protein 33g, Carbs 2g

Ingredients:

- 4 eggs
- 1 cup coconut milk
- 1/4 cup chia seeds
- 1 cup spinach, chopped
- 1/2 tsp black pepper
- 1/2 tsp ground nutmeg
- 1 tsp baking soda
- 1/2 cup coconut flour
- 1/2 tsp salt

Instructions:

- In a bowl, whisk eggs with coconut milk until frothy.
- Mix together all dry ingredients and add in the egg mixture and whisk until smooth.
- Add spinach and stir well.
- Preheat the griddle to medium-low heat.
- Spray griddle top with cooking spray.
- Pour 3–4 tbsp of batter onto the hot griddle top and make a round pancake.
- Cook pancake until lightly golden brown from both sides.
- Serve and enjoy..

Burgers Recipes

Lamb and Cucumber Burger

(**Preparation time:** 5 minutes | **Cooking time:** 5 minutes | **Servings:** 4)

Per serving: Calories 635; Fat 23.7g; Sodium 616mg; Carbs 11.1g; Fiber 1.6g; Sugar 0.6g; Protein 89g

Ingredients:

- 1¼ pounds lean ground lamb
- tablespoon ground cumin
- ¼ teaspoon ground cinnamon
- ½ teaspoon salt
- ½ teaspoon freshly ground black pepper
- whole wheat pitas
- ½ medium cucumber, peeled and sliced
- ½ cup Simple Garlic Yogurt Sauce

Instructions:

- Combine the lamb, cumin, cinnamon, salt, and black pepper in a medium mixing basin. Mix the seasonings into the meat with a fork, then form the mixture into four 1-inch-thick patties with your hands.
- Set the Griddle to high heat, then place the burgers on the griddle and cook for 5 minutes without flipping.
- Remove the burgers and keep them covered to keep them heated.
- Place a burger in each pita, along with a few cucumber slices and a dollop of the yoghurt sauce on top.
- Serve right away.

Marinated Portobello Cheese Burgers

(**Preparation time:** 10 minutes | **Cooking time:** 10 minutes | **Servings:** 4)

Per serving: Calories 254; Fat 14 g; Sodium 496mg; Carbs 24.6g; Fiber 1.6g; Sugar 3.6g; Protein 13g

Ingredients:

- 4 Portobello mushroom caps
- 4 slices mozzarella cheese

- 4 buns, like brioche
- For the marinade:
- ¼ cup balsamic vinegar
- 2 tablespoons olive oil
- 1 teaspoon dried basil
- 1 teaspoon dried oregano
- 1 teaspoon garlic powder
- ¼ teaspoon sea salt
- ¼ teaspoon black pepper

Instructions:

- Whip together the marinade ingredients in a huge mixing bowl. Toss the mushroom caps in the sauce to coat them.
- Preheat the griddle to medium-high temperature.
- Place the mushrooms on the griddle and keep the marinade aside for basting.
- Cook the meat for 5–8 minutes on each side, or until done.
- Brush the marinade on the meat on a regular basis.
- Sprinkle mozzarella cheese on top during the last 2 minutes of cooking.
- Serve the brioche buns straight from the griddle.

Croque Ham Cheese Burgers

(**Preparation time:** 10 minutes | **Cooking time:** 10 minutes | **Servings:** 2)

Per serving: Calories 475; Fat 30 g; Sodium 641 mg; Carbs 24.6g; Fiber 3.6g; Sugar 4.1g; Protein 26.1g **Ingredients:**

- 2 tablespoons butter
- 1 tablespoon flour
- ⅔ cup milk
- 2 slices thick cut bread
- 2 slices black forest ham
- 2 slices gruyere cheese
- Salt and black pepper
- 2 eggs
- Béchamel sauce, as you like

Instructions:

- In a small pan over medium heat, melt one tablespoon of butter before stirring in the flour. After whisking until just just browned, add the milk.

- Stirring should continue until the sauce thickens. As soon as you take the food from the stove, season with salt and pepper.
- the griddle to medium heat.
- Each piece of bread should have one side buttered and the other generously covered with béchamel sauce.
- Two slices of ham and the final piece of bread are placed on top of each sandwich. Cook the pancakes on the griddle until golden brown.
- Place the gruyere cheese on top of the sandwiches and flip them over.
- Crack the eggs on the other side of the griddle and cook until the whites are set.
- Cook until the gruyere on top has melted and the other side of the sandwich is golden brown. Before serving, place a fried egg on top of each sandwich.

Beef and Corn Burgers

(**Preparation time:** 20 minutes | **Cooking time:** 30 minutes | **Servings:** 6)

Per serving: Calories 266, Total fat 14g, Protein 33g, Carbs 2g

Ingredients:

- 1 large egg, lightly beaten
- 1 cup whole kernel corn, cooked
- ½ cup bread crumbs
- 2 tablespoons shallots, minced
- 1 teaspoon Worcestershire sauce
- 2 pounds ground beef
- 1 teaspoon salt
- ½ teaspoon pepper
- ½ teaspoon ground sage

Instructions:

- Whisk together the egg, corn, bread crumbs, shallots, and Worcestershire sauce in a mixing bowl.
- Combine the ground beef and the remaining seasonings in a separate bowl.
- Cover a level surface with waxed paper.
- From the meat mixture, make 12 thin burger patties.

- Fill the centre of each of the 6 patties with the corn mixture and spread evenly to within an inch of the edge.
- To seal the corn mixture in the middle, place a second circle of meat on top of each burger and push the edges together.
- Over medium heat, griddle for 12-15 minutes on each side, or until thermometer reads 160°F and juices run clear.

Bulgur Beet Burgers

(**Preparation time:** 5 minutes | **Cooking time:** 10 minutes | **Servings:** 6)

Per serving: Calories 266, Total fat 14g, Protein 33g, Carbs 2g

Ingredients:

- 1 pound beets, peeled and grated (about 2 cups) ½ cup packed pitted dates, broken into pieces ½ cup almonds
- 1 teaspoon ginger powder
- ½ cup bulgur
- Salt and pepper
- ¾ cup boiling red wine or water
- 1 tablespoon Dijon or other mustard
- Cayenne or red chili flakes (optional)

Instructions:

- In a food processor, pulse the beets, dates, almonds, and ginger powder until finely minced but not quite a paste.
- Add the bulgur and a pinch of salt and pepper to the mixture in a large mixing bowl. Cover the bowl with a plate and stir in the boiling wine, mustard, and cayenne to taste if using.
- Allow the bulgur to soften for 20 minutes.
- Season with salt and pepper to taste. Refrigerate for at least 1 hour after shaping into ½ burgers and placing on a tray without touching.
- When the griddle is heated, turn the control knob to high and set the burgers on it. Cook for 10 minutes without rotating.
- Serve with the fixings or toppings of your choice.

Marinated Portobello Cheese Burgers

(**Preparation time:** 05 minutes| **Cook time:** 10 minutes| **Serves:** 2)

Per Serving: Calories 254, Fat 14 g, Sodium 496mg, Carbs 24.6g, Fiber 1.6g, Sugar 3.6g, Protein 13g

Ingredients:

- 4 Portobello mushroom caps
- 4 slices mozzarella cheese
- 4 buns, like brioche

For the marinade:

- ¼ cup balsamic vinegar
- 2 tablespoons olive oil
- 1 teaspoon dried basil
- 1 teaspoon dried oregano
- 1 teaspoon garlic powder
- ¼ teaspoon sea salt
- ¼ teaspoon black pepper

Istructions:

- Whip together the marinade ingredients in a huge mixing bowl. Toss the mushroom caps in the sauce to coat them.
- Set aside at room temperature for 15 minutes, rotating twice.
- Preheat the griddle to medium-high temperature.
- Place the mushrooms on the griddle and keep the marinade aside for basting.
- Cook the meat for 5–8 minutes on each side, or until done.
- Brush the marinade on the meat on a regular basis.
- Sprinkle mozzarella cheese on top during the last 2 minutes of cooking.
- Serve the brioche buns straight from the griddle.

Garlic Parsley Cheese Sandwiches

(**Preparation time:** 2 minutes| **Cook time:** 7 minutes| **Serves:** 1)

Per Serving: Calories 555; Fat 44.7 g; Sodium 1034mg; Carbs 14.6g; Fiber 1g; Sugar 1.2g; Protein 25.8g

Ingredients:

- 2 slices Italian bread, sliced thin
- 2 slices provolone cheese
- 2 tablespoons butter, softened
- Garlic powder, for dusting

- Dried parsley, for dusting
- Parmesan Cheese, shredded, for dusting

Istructions:

- Spread butter evenly across 2 slices of bread and season with garlic and parsley on each greased side.
- Spread a few teaspoons of Parmesan cheese over each greased side of the bread and gently press it in.
- Preheat the griddle to medium heat and set one slice of bread on the griddle, buttered side down.
- Top with provolone slices and a butter-side-up second slice of bread.
- Cook for 3 minutes on one side, then flip and cook for another 3 minutes, or until bread is golden and parmesan cheese is crunchy.
- Serve immediately with your favorite side dishes!

Turkey Burger Patty Melts

(**Preparation time:** 15 minutes | **Cooking time:** 10 minutes | **Servings:** 6)

Per serving: Calories: 278; Total Fat: 9 g; Cholesterol: 63 mg; Carbohydrates: 16 g; Protein: 23 g

Ingredients:

- 2 pounds turkey burger patties, frozen, cooked and crumbled 1/4 cup fat-free mayonnaise
- 2 teaspoons prepared horseradish
- 6 slices (about 1/4 inch thick) or 12 slices (1/8 inch thick) sourdough bread; toasted

Instructions:

- In a large bowl, combine onion, mustard, ketchup, mayonnaise and horseradish. Stir in crumbled burger patties.
- Arrange bread slices on a work surface. Spoon 1/4 of the turkey mixture over each slice of bread. Sprinkle with cheese and top with the second slice of bread.
- Heat a griddle over medium heat until hot enough for a drop of water to bounce on it. Cook sandwiches for about 3 to 5 minutes or until golden brown and cheese is melted, turning once. Serve hot immediately.

Garlicky Pork Burgers

(**Preparation time:** 5 minutes | **Cooking time:** 10 minutes | **Servings:** 2)

Per serving: Calories 154; Fat 8g; Sodium 781mg; Carbs 18.3g; Fiber 1.6g; Sugar 3.1g; Protein 4.3g

Ingredients:

- ½ teaspoon salt
- ½ teaspoon black pepper
- 2 cloves garlic, chopped
- 2 hard rolls

Instructions:

- In a food processor, pulse the meat, salt, pepper, and garlic until coarsely ground, but not much finer than chopped. (If using pre-ground beef, add it in a mixing dish with the salt, pepper, and garlic and mix gently with your hands.)
- To prevent crushing the meat, shape it into four 1- to 112-inch thick burgers with as little manipulation as possible. (You can make this ahead of time and keep it refrigerated until you're ready to griddle it.) Set the Griddle to high heat and place the burgers on it; cook for 10 minutes without flipping; the internal temperature should be 160°F
- Serve on a serving platter.
- In the oven, warm the rolls.
- Serve the patties on a slice of bread.

Cheese and Tomato Burgers

(**Preparation time:** 10 minutes | **Cooking time:** 10 minutes | **Servings:** 4)

Per serving: Calories 518; Fat 30.3g; Sodium 976 mg; Carbs 40.3g; Fiber 1.6g; Sugar 3.1g; Protein 22g

Ingredients:

- 8 slices sourdough bread
- 4 slices provolone cheese
- 4 slices yellow American cheese
- 4 slices sharp cheddar cheese
- 4 slices tomato
- 3 tablespoons mayonnaise
- 3 tablespoons butter

Instructions:

- Preheat the griddle to medium-high heat.
- Spread mayo on one side of each slice of bread and butter the other.

- Arrange the cheeses on top of the buttered side of the griddle.
- Place the other slices of bread on top of the cheese, butter side up.
- Cook for 10 minutes, flipping halfway through, until the other piece of bread is golden brown and the cheese has melted.
- Take it from the griddle, slice it in half, and eat.

Vegetables and Side Dishes Recipes

Italian Zucchini Slices

(**Preparation time:** 10 minutes | **Cooking time:** 10 minutes | **Servings:** 4)

Per serving: Calories: 238.78 Fat: 17.1 g Fiber: 3 g Protein: 17.5 g

Ingredients:

- 2 zucchini, cut into 1/2-inch thick slices 1 teaspoon Italian seasoning
- 2 garlic cloves, minced
- 1/4 cup butter, melted
- 1 1/2 tablespoons fresh parsley, chopped
- 1 tablespoon fresh lemon juice
- Pepper
- Salt

Instructions:

- In a small bowl, put together melted butter, lemon juice, Italian seasoning, garlic, pepper, and salt.
- Brush zucchini slices with melted butter mixture.
- Preheat the griddle to high heat.
- Place zucchini slices on the griddle top and cook for 2 minutes per side.
- Transfer zucchini slices to serving plate and garnish with parsley. Serve and enjoy.

Vegetable Skewers

(**Preparation time:** 20 minutes | **Cooking time:** 14 minutes | **Servings:** 4)

Ingredients:

- 1 Red Pepper, cubed
- 1 zucchini, sliced
- 1 yellow or summer squash, sliced
- 10 Bella mushrooms
- 1 Red Onion Diced
- Oil
- Seasonings

Instructions:

- To begin, soak your wooden skewers for around 10 minutes in water.

- Then warm the griddle for about 5 minutes on medium-high heat.
- Brush or massage the oil over the veggies and season them while the griddle is preheating. They should be threaded through the skewers.
- Cook for 10 to 14 minutes on the griddle with the veggie skewer.
- During the cooking phase, flipping is often done. If you need extra oil, add it along with some spices.
- Plate, serve, and have a good time!

Vegetable Yakisoba

(**Preparation time:** 10 minutes | **Cooking time:** 15 minutes | **Servings:** 8)

Per serving: Calories 266, Total fat 14g, Protein 33g, Carbs 2g

Ingredients:

Sauce

- 2 tbsp soy sauce
- 4 tbsp water
- 2 tbsp mirin
- 1 tsp sesame oil
- 2 tsp minced garlic
- 2 tsp chili garlic sauce
- 1 tsp sriracha
- 2 tbsp brown sugar
- 1/2 tsp ground ginger
- 1 tbsp cornstarch
- 1 tsp canola oil

Stir-Fry

- 3-4 tbsp oil
- 1/2 cup of sliced onions
- 1 sliced bell pepper
- 1 cup of chopped broccoli
- 1 cup of sliced zucchini
- 1/2 cup of matchstick carrots
- 1 handful of baby spinach (optional)
- 17 ounces of fresh yakisoba noodles

Instructions:

- To make the sauce, add all of the ingredients to a mixing bowl and whisk to incorporate. Set aside.
- Preheat your griddle to medium-high heat, add 1 tbsp of oil and a splash of sesame oil to the griddle, and immediately stir-fry the vegetables until they are crisp-tender (about 3-4 minutes). Remove the griddle from the heat, cover it, and put it aside.
- Preheat the griddle with the remaining tbsp of oil and toss in the noodles, vegetables, and shrimp. Pour in the sauce after a minute of stirring.
- Stir until the sauce has thickened, keeping as much of it with the noodles as possible (and not running into the oil bucket), and serve right away.

Grilled Vegetables

(**Preparation time:** 15 minutes | **Cooking time:** 30 minutes | **Servings:** 4)

Per serving: Calories 266, Total fat 14g, Protein 33g, Carbs 2g

Ingredients:

- 2 sliced zucchini
- 2 sliced yellow squash
- 1 (cut into cubes) red pepper
- 1 Pound halved mushroom
- 1 halved and sliced onion
- 2 cups of broccoli florets
- 2 cups of cauliflower florets
- lightly sprinkle with olive oil
- 3 tbsp fresh lemon juice
- 8 garlic cloves
- 1 tbsp chopped fresh basil
- ¼ cup of chopped parsley
- ½tsp oregano
- salt
- pepper

Instructions:

- 2 large sheets of heavy-duty tin foil, layered 2. add vegetables.
- Toss together the dressing ingredients and sprinkle over the veggies.
- Fold the tin foil in half and seal it securely.
- Cover and grill for 30 minutes over medium heat, flipping the package once.
- Cut the foil into pieces and serve.

Fried Rice on the Griddle

(**Preparation time:** 10 minutes | **Cooking time:** 10 minutes | **Servings:** 2)

Ingredients:

- 2 cups of white rice
- 1 every minced Carrot
- 1 chopped onion
- 1 cup of fresh peas
- 1 tbsp minced garlic
- 4 every egg
- 1 few drops of sesame oil
- 1 few drops of soy sauce
- 1 few drops of oyster sauce (optional)

Instructions:

- Begin by cooking two cups of cold white rice. We like Jasmine rice, but any rice would suffice.
- Carrots, onions, peas, and garlic should be sautéed on a well-oiled griddle over high heat. Remove from heat.
- Pour the mixture onto the griddle after whisking an egg with a few drops of toasted sesame oil. Wait for it to puff up, then flip it and cut it.
- Return to the griddle after adding the vegetables to the cold rice.
- Cook until the rice is warm, then add a few drops of soy sauce, oyster sauce, and toasted sesame oil.
- Remove the griddle from the heat, add the scrambled egg, and serve.

Lemon Garlic Artichokes

(**Preparation time:** 10 minutes | **Cooking time:** 15 minutes | **Servings:** 4)

Per serving: Calcium: 47 mg Magnesium: 39 mg Phosphorus: 344 mg Iron: 2.77 mg Potassium: 575 mg Sodium: 98 mg Zinc: 7.04 mg

Ingredients:

- 1/2 lemon Juice
- 1/2 cup canola oil
- 3 garlic cloves, chopped
- Sea salt
- Freshly ground black pepper
- 2 large artichokes, trimmed and halved

Instructions:

- Preheat the griddle to medium high.
- Lemon juice, oil, and garlic should be combined in a medium bowl while the appliance is preheating. Sprinkle the artichoke halves with salt and pepper before brushing over the lemon-garlic mixture.
- Place the artichokes on the griddle, cut side down. Gently press them down. Cook for 8 to 10 minutes, occasionally basting generously with the lemon-garlic mixture throughout cooking, until blistered on all sides.

Blistered Green Beans

(**Preparation time:** 10 minutes | **Cooking time:** 10 minutes | **Servings:** 4)

Per serving: Calcium: 55 mg Magnesium: 47 mg Phosphorus: 363 mg Iron: 3.11 mg Potassium: 701 mg Sodium: 198 mg Zinc: 7.02 mg

Ingredients:

- 1 pound haricots verts or green beans, trimmed
- 2 tablespoons vegetable oil
- Juice of 1 lemon
- Pinch red pepper flakes
- Flaky sea salt
- Freshly ground black pepper

Instructions:

- Preheat the griddle to medium-high. While the unit is preheating, in a medium bowl, toss the green beans in oil until evenly coated.
- Place the green beans on the griddle, and cook for 8 to 10 minutes, tossing frequently until blistered on all sides. When cooking is complete, place the green beans on a large serving platter.
- Squeeze lemon juice over the green beans, top with red pepper flakes, and season with sea salt and black pepper.

Steamed Carrots in Ranch Dressing

(**Preparetion time:** 15 minutes | **Cook time:** 20 minutes | **Serves:** 5)

Per Serving: Calories 304, Fat 14.9g, Sodium 304mg, Carbs 12g, Fiber 6g, Sugar 2g, Protein 21g

Ingredients:

- 12 petite carrots
- 1 packet dry ranch dressing/seasoning mix
- 2 olive oil
- Water

Istructions:

- Grease the cooking surface of the griddle with cooking spray.
- Turn on the 4 burners and turn their knobs to medium heat.
- Let the Griddle preheat for 5 minutes.
- In a suitable bowl, combine carrots, olive oil and ranch seasoning mix,.
- Stir until well-combined and all the carrots are coated evenly with oil and seasoning.
- Add carrots to the griddle and then let it cook for almost 3 minutes, with occasional stirring.
- Add 3 tablespoons water to the pile of carrots to generate steam.
- Cover carrot pile with basting cover or similar metal dish.
- Toss carrots, add 2-3 tablespoons water, and re-cover with basting marinade to continue steaming.
- Cook carrots for approximately 12 minutes or to desired tenderness.
- Serve.

Zucchini Squash Mix

(Preparation time: 15 minutes | **Cook time:** 10 minutes | **Serves:** 6)

Per Serving: Calories 381, Fat 21g, Sodium 561mg, Carbs 21g, Fiber 6.1g, Sugar 5g, Protein 32g

Ingredients:

- 2 zucchini, diced
- 2 squash, diced
- 1 large onion, diced
- 2-3 tomatoes on the vine, diced
- 5-6 garlic cloves, roughly chopped
- 1 can cannelloni beans, drained
- Olive oil
- Black pepper and salt to taste

Istructions:

- Toss all the veggies and beans with black pepper and salt in a suitable bowl.
- Grease the cooking surface of the griddle with cooking spray.

- Turn on the 4 burners and turn their knobs to medium heat.
- Let the Griddle preheat for 5 minutes.
- Add the veggie mixture to the griddle top and then let it cook until soft.
- Serve.

Sautéed Savoury Green Beans

(**Preparation time:** 15 minutes | **Cook time:** 20 minutes | **Serves:** 6)

Per Serving: Calories 339, Fat 13g; Sodium 421mg, Carbs 16g, Fiber 4.1g, Sugar 3.2g, Protein 27g

Ingredients:

- 2 lbs. fresh green beans
- 1 tablespoon of olive oil
- 1 teaspoon of garlic powder
- Black pepper and salt to taste

Istructions:

- In a suitable bowl, mix all the recipe's ingredients until beans are well-coated.
- Grease the cooking surface of the griddle with cooking spray.
- Turn on the 4 burners and turn their knobs to medium-high heat.
- Let the Griddle preheat for 5 minutes.
- Spread the beans on the griddles and then let it cook for 20 minutes with stirring.
- Serve.
- Cook beans on griddle until they reach desired tenderness, with occasional stirring.

Easy Seared Green Beans

(**Preparation time:** 10 minutes | **Cooking time:** 10 minutes | **Servings:** 6)

Per serving: Calories 266, Total fat 14g, Protein 33g, Carbs 2g

Ingredients:

- 1 1/2 lbs green beans, trimmed
- 1 1/2 tablespoons rice vinegar
- 3 tablespoons soy sauce
- 1 1/2 tablespoons sesame oil
- 2 tablespoons sesame seeds, toasted
- 1 1/2 tablespoons brown sugar
- 1/4 teaspoons black pepper

Instructions:

- Cook beans for 3 minutes and drain well.
- Transfer green beans to chilled ice water and drain again. Pat dry green beans.
- Preheat the griddle to high heat.
- Add oil to the hot griddle top.
- Add green beans and stir fry for 2 minutes.
- Add soy sauce, brown sugar, vinegar, and pepper and stir fry for 2
- minutes more.
- Add sesame seeds and toss well to coat. Serve and enjoy.

Grilled Hash Browns

(**Preparation time:** 10 minutes | **Cooking time:** 30 minutes | **Servings:** 4)

Ingredients:

- 4 Tbsp unsalted softened butter
- 20 Ounces shredded hash brown potatoes thawed if frozen 1 large seeded and diced green bell pepper ½ cup of diced white or yellow onion
- 2 cloves garlic minced or chopped
- ½ tsp kosher salt
- ¼ tsp fresh cracked pepper
- 4 large eggs
- garnish: chopped flat-leaf parsley

Instructions:

- Get the griddle ready clean, and season the griddle before using it.
- Reduce the heat to medium once everything is ready.
- To take to the griddle, mix all of the ingredients on a tray. In a mixing dish, mix the potatoes, green bell pepper, onion, and garlic.
- On the griddle, melt the butter. The griddle should be heated enough for the butter to melt rapidly and sizzle but not burn.
- Toss in the potatoes, green bell pepper, onion, and garlic with the potatoes, green bell pepper, onion, and garlic to coat. Cook, often flipping, until the potatoes are lightly browned and almost (but not quite) cooked through (about 5 minutes). Take care not to toss the potatoes too much since they need to brown immediately on the hot griddle. Check for doneness with a taste every now and then.
- After seasoning with salt and pepper, assemble the potatoes into a 12-

- inch-wide mound. Make four wells in the potatoes using a fork or a spoon. Crack an egg into every well gently. Cook covered with a frying dome.
- Serve immediately with a parsley garnish.

Crispy Cooked Potatoes

(**Preparation time:** 15 minutes | **Cooking time:** 25 minutes | **Servings:** 6)

Per serving: Calories 416; Fat 11g; Sodium 501mg; Carbs 16g; Fiber 2.1g; Sugar 2.2g; Protein 28g

Ingredients:

- 6 potatoes, diced
- 2 tablespoons olive oil
- 2 teaspoons of black pepper
- 2 ½ teaspoons of garlic powder
- 2 teaspoons of dried rosemary
- Salt to taste

Instructions:

In a suitable pot, boil sliced potatoes until fork tender.

Transfer potatoes from water into a suitable bowl.

Add olive oil, garlic powder, black pepper, rosemary, and salt.

Toss until potatoes are evenly coated.

Grease the cooking surface of the griddle with cooking spray.

Turn on the 4 burners and turn their knobs to medium heat.

Let the Griddle preheat for 5 minutes.

Add potatoes to griddle and then let it cook for 5-6 minutes each side or until crispy.

Serve.

Parmesan Zucchini

(**Preparation time:** 15 minutes | **Cooking time:** 15 minutes | **Servings:** 4)

Per serving: Calories 338; Fat 12g; Sodium 521mg; Carbs 14g; Fiber 5.1g; Sugar 3g; Protein 27g

Ingredients:

- 3 medium zucchinis, sliced
- 1 tablespoon of olive oil
- 1 tablespoon of grated parmesan cheese
- ½ teaspoon of garlic powder
- ¼ teaspoon of black pepper

Instructions:

- Grease the cooking surface of the griddle with cooking spray.
- Turn on the 4 burners and turn their knobs to medium heat.
- Let the Griddle preheat for 5 minutes.
- Add sliced zucchini then cook for about 3 minutes, with occasional stirring.
- Add parmesan cheese, garlic powder, and pepper and continue sautéing until zucchini is tender.
- Serve.

Fried Green Tomatoes with Parsley

(**Preparation time:** 10 minutes | **Cooking time:** 10 minutes | **Servings:** 1)

Per serving: Calories 304; Fat 14.9g; Sodium 304mg; Carbs 12g; Fiber 6g; Sugar 2g; Protein 21g

Ingredients:

- 4 green tomatoes
- 3 cups of Italian style bread crumbs
- 2 cups of flour
- 2 teaspoons of garlic powder
- 3 eggs
- ½ cup of milk
- Black pepper and salt to taste
- Parsley garnish, chopped
- Lemon zest garnish
- 3 tablespoons of butter
- 2 ½ tablespoons of flour

Instructions:

- Beat 3 eggs with ½ cup of milk, black pepper and salt in a suitable bowl.
- Mix 2 cups flour with 2 teaspoon garlic powder in another.
- Spread Italian seasoned bread crumbs in a plate.
- Slice tomatoes ¼ to a ½ inch thick

- Coat the slices in the flour mixture evenly and shaking off any excess flour.
- Then dip and coat evenly in the egg wash, then into the breadcrumb, pressing slices into the crumbs.
- Grease the cooking surface of the griddle with cooking spray.
- Turn on the 4 burners and turn their knobs to medium heat.
- Let the Griddle preheat for 5 minutes.
- Place the coated tomato slices on the griddle top and then let it cook for 5
- minutes per side.
- Serve.

Tasty Cornish Game Hen

(**Preparation time:** 10 minutes | **Cooking time:** 10 minutes | **Servings:** 4)

Per serving: Calories 378; Fat 15g; Sodium 521mg; Carbs 14g; Fiber 5.1g; Sugar 3g; Protein 27g

Ingredients:

- 1 Cornish game hen
- ½ tablespoons of olive oil
- ¼ tablespoon of poultry seasoning

Instructions:

- Grease the cooking surface of the griddle with cooking spray.
- Turn on the 4 burners and turn their knobs to medium-high heat.
- Let the Griddle preheat for 5 minutes.
- Brush hen with oil and rub with poultry seasoning.
- Place hen on preheated griddle top and then let it cook from all the sides until brown.
- Cover hen with lid or pan and smoke for 60 minutes or until the internal temperature of hen reaches 180°F.
- Serve.

Poultry Recipes

California Seared Chicken

(**Preparation time:** 35 minutes | **Cooking time:** 20 minutes | **Servings:** 4)

Per serving: Calories: 230 Protein: 37.5 g Carbs: 2.2 g Fat: 7 g Sugar: 1.3 g

Ingredients:

- 4 boneless, skinless chicken breasts
- 3/4 cup balsamic vinegar
- 2 tablespoons extra virgin olive oil
- 1 tablespoon honey
- 1 teaspoon oregano
- 1 teaspoon basil
- 1 teaspoon garlic powder
- For garnish:
- Sea salt to taste
- Black pepper, fresh ground to taste
- 4 slices fresh mozzarella cheese
- 4 slices avocado
- 4 slices beefsteak tomato
- Balsamic glaze, for drizzling

Instructions:

- In a large mixing bowl, combine the balsamic vinegar, honey, olive oil, oregano, basil, and garlic powder.
- Chicken should be added after coating, then marinated for 30 minutes in the fridge.
- Furnish griddle with medium-high heat. 7 minutes each side, or until a meat thermometer registers 165°F
- , should be used to sear chicken.
- Each chicken breast should have mozzarella, avocado, and tomato on top. Cover the griddle with foil to allow the cheese to melt for two minutes.
- Add a drizzle of balsamic glaze, some sea salt, and some black pepper for garnish.

Chili Lime Chicken with Sesame Seed

(**Preparetion time:** 35 minutes | **Cook time:** 15 minutes | **Serves:** 4)

Per Serving: Calories 950| Fat 33.7 g| Sodium 1541 mg| Carbs 18.4g| Fiber 0.2g| Sugar 16g| Protein 132.2g

Ingredients:

- ½ cup sweet chili sauce
- ¼ cup soy sauce
- 1-teaspoon mirin
- ½-teaspoon orange juice
- 1-teaspoon orange marmelade
- 1-tablespoon lime juice
- 1 tbsp. brown sugar
- 1 clove garlic, minced
- 4-pound Boneless chicken breasts
- Sesame seeds, for garnish

Istructions:

- In a suitable mixing bowl, combine soy sauce, brown sugar, sweet chili sauce, orange marmalade, mirin, lime and orange juice, and minced garlic.
- Reserve ¼ cup of this orange sauce.
- Add the chicken to the remaining sauce, mix well to coat and set aside for 30
- minutes to marinate.
- Preheat the Griddle by turning all its knob to medium-heat setting.
- Grease the griddle top with cooking spray.
- Place the chicken on the hot griddle top and cook for 7 minutes per side.
- Garnish with sesame seeds and serve.

Seared Spicy Boneless Chicken Thighs

(Preparetion time: 8-24 hours | **Cook time:** 20 minutes | **Serves:** 4)

Per Serving: Calories 559| Fat 23.8 g| Sodium 430 mg| Carbs 18.3g| Fiber 0.3g| Sugar 17.6g| Protein 65.8g

Ingredients:

- 2-pound boneless chicken thighs
- ¼ cup fresh lime juice
- 2-teaspoon lime zest
- ¼ cup honey
- 2 tablespoons olive oil
- ½-tablespoon balsamic vinegar

- ½-teaspoon sea salt
- ½-teaspoon black pepper
- ½ Garlic cloves, minced
- ¼-teaspoon onion powder

Istructions:

- In a suitable mixing bowl, whisk all marinade ingredients; keep 2 tablespoons of the marinade for basting.
- Mix the chicken with marinade in a sealable plastic bag, shake and refrigerate overnight.
- Preheat the Griddle by turning all its knob to medium-heat setting.
- Grease the griddle top with cooking oil.
- Cook the marinated chicken for 8 minutes per side while basting on the hot griddle top.
- Serve and enjoy!

Honey Balsamic Marinated Chicken

(**Preparation time:** 30 minutes – 4 hours | **Cooking time:** 20 minutes | **Servings:** 4)

Per serving: Calories: 485 Sodium: 438 mg Dietary Fiber: 0.5 g Fat: 18.1 g Carbs: 11 g Protein: 66.1 g

Ingredients:

- 2 lbs. boneless, skinless chicken thighs
- 1 teaspoon olive oil
- 1/2 teaspoon sea salt
- 1/4 teaspoon black pepper
- 1/2 teaspoon paprika
- 3/4 teaspoon onion powder
- For the Marinade:
- 2 tablespoons honey
- 2 tablespoons balsamic vinegar
- 2 tablespoons tomato paste
- 1 teaspoon garlic, minced

Instructions:

- Add chicken, olive oil, salt, black pepper, paprika, and onion powder to a sealable plastic bag. Seal and toss to coat, covering the chicken with spices and oil; set aside.
- Whisk together balsamic vinegar, tomato paste, garlic, and honey.
- Divide the marinade in half. Add one half to the bag of chicken and store the other half in a sealed container in the refrigerator.

- Seal the bag and toss chicken to coat. Refrigerate for 30 minutes to 4
- hours.
- Preheat a griddle to medium-high.
- Discard bag and marinade. Add chicken to the griddle and cook 7
- minutes per side and a meat thermometer reads 165°F
- Serve immediately.

Glazed Chicken Wings

(**Preparation time**: 15 minutes | **Cook time**: 30 minutes | **Serves**: 4)

Per Serving: Calories 914, Fat 49.5 g, Sodium 1398 mg, Carbs 67.7g, Fiber 1.1g, Sugar 38.2g, Protein 45.3g

Ingredients:

- 1 (12 oz.) Jar peach pre*Serves:*
- 1 cup sweet red chili sauce
- 1-teaspoon lime juice
- 1 tbsp. fresh cilantro, minced
- 1 (2-½-pound) bag chicken wing sections
- Non-stick cooking spray

Istructions:

- In a suitable mixing bowl, mix the pre*Serves:*, lime juice, red chili sauce, and cilantro.
- Divide this mixture in half and set aside one half for serving.
- Preheat the Griddle by turning all its knob to medium-heat setting.
- Grease the griddle top with cooking spray.
- Cook wings on the hot griddle top for 25 minutes, flipping every 5 minutes.
- Toss them with ½ of the glaze and cook for 3 minutes more on high heat.
- Serve with left over glaze.
-

Herb Roasted Turkey in Chicken Broth

(**Preparation time**: 15 minutes | **Cook** time: 3 hrs. 35 minutes | **Serves**: 12)

Per Serving: Calories 376; Fat 13g; Sodium 421mg; Carbs 16g; Fiber 4.1g; Sugar 3.2g; Protein 27g

Ingredients:

Fourteen pounds of turkey, cleaned

2 tablespoons of chopped mixed herbs

¼ teaspoon of ground black pepper, to taste

3 tablespoons of butter, unsalted, melted

2 cups of chicken broth

Istructions:

- Grease the cooking surface of the griddle with cooking spray.
- Turn on the 4 burners and turn their knobs to medium heat.
- Let the Griddle preheat for 5 minutes.
- Remove the giblets from the turkey, wash it inside and out, then wipe it dry with paper towels before placing it on a roasting pan and tucking the turkey wings with butcher's thread.
- Meanwhile, make herb butter by placing melted butter in a suitable bowl, adding black pepper and mixed herbs, and whisking until frothy.
- Using the handle of a wooden spoon, place some of the prepared herb butter beneath the skin of the turkey and massage the skin to evenly spread the butter.
- Then massage melted butter all over the outside of the turkey, season with pork and poultry rub, and pour the liquid into the roasting pan.
- When the griddle is hot, remove the cover, lay the roasting pan with the turkey on the griddle grate, close the griddle, and smoke for 3 hours and 30
- minutes, or until the internal temperature reaches 165 degrees F and the top is golden brown.
- When the turkey is done, take it to a cutting board and let it rest for 30
- minutes before carving it into slices and serving it.
- Serve.

Butterflied Chicken

(Preparation time: 15 minutes | **Cooking time:** 50 minutes | **Servings:** 6)

Per serving: Calories 507, Total Fat 17.1 g, Saturated Fat 4 g, Cholesterol 227 mg, Sodium 162 mg, Total Carbs 0.8 g, Fiber 0.1 g, Sugar 0.1 g, Protein 82.2 g

Ingredients:

- 1 (3½-4-pound) whole chicken, neck and giblets removed 3 tablespoons fresh lime juice
- 2 tablespoons extra-virgin olive oil
- 1 tablespoon garlic, minced
- 2 teaspoons lime zest, freshly grated 3 tablespoons Mexican chili powder
- 1 teaspoon ground coriander
- 1 teaspoon ground cumin
- Salt and ground black pepper, as required

Instructions:

- Arrange the chicken onto a large cutting board, breast side down.
- With kitchen shears, start from thigh and cut along 1 side of the backbone and turn the chicken around.
- Now, cut along the other side and discard the backbone.
- Change the side and open it like a book and then flatten the backbone firmly.
- In a clean glass bowl, blend together lime juice, oil, garlic, lime zest, chile powder, coriander, cumin, salt and black pepper.
- Coat the chicken evenly with spice mixture.
- Cover the chicken with plastic wrap and refrigerator for about 24
- hours.
- Preheat half of the Outdoor Gas Griddle to medium-high heat and leave the remaining half of griddle unheated.
- Place the chicken with the marinade on the preheated griddle, skin side down and cook for about 5 minutes.
- Flip the chicken and cook for about 5 minutes.
- Now place the chicken onto the unheated side of the griddle and cover with the cooking dome.
- Cook for about 30-40 minutes or until done completely.
- Remove from the griddle and place the chicken onto a platter for about 10 minutes before carving.
- Cut the chicken into desired sized pieces and serve.

Lemony Chicken Breast

(**Preparation time:** 15 minutes | **Cooking time:** 16 minutes | **Servings:** 6)

Per serving: Calories 434, Total Fat 28.1 g, Saturated Fat 5.6 g, Cholesterol 135 mg, Sodium 159 mg, Total Carbs 0.4 g, Fiber 0.1 g, Sugar 0.2 g, Protein 43.9 g

Ingredients:

- ½ cup olive oil
- ¼ cup fresh lemon juice
- 1 garlic clove, minced
- Salt and ground black pepper, as required
- 2 pounds boneless, skinless chicken breasts

Instructions:

- For marinade: in a large bowl, add the oil, lemon juice, garlic, salt, and black pepper and beat until well combined.
- Place the chicken breasts and marinade into a large resealable plastic bag.
- Seal bag and shake to coat well.
- Refrigerate overnight.
- Preheat the Outdoor Gas Griddle to medium heat.
- Grease the griddle generously.
- Remove the chicken breasts from bag and discard the marinade.
- Place the chicken breasts onto the griddle and cover with a cooking dome.
- Cook for about 6-8 minutes per side.
- Serve hot.

Sweet and Spicy Chicken Breast

(**Preparation time:** 15 minutes | **Cooking time:** 20 minutes | **Servings:** 4)

Per serving: Calories 329, Total Fat 17.9 g, Saturated Fat 3.7 g, Cholesterol 82 mg, Sodium 933 mg, Total Carbs 10.2 g, Fiber 0.5 g, Sugar 7.3 g, Protein 33.1 g

Ingredients:

- 4 skinless, boneless chicken breasts
- 1 (1-inch) piece fresh ginger, minced
- 2 garlic cloves, minced
- 1 cup fresh pineapple juice
- ¼ cup low-sodium soy sauce
- ¼ cup extra-virgin olive oil
- 1 teaspoon ground cinnamon
- 1 teaspoon ground cumin
- Salt, as required

Instructions:

- In a plastic zippered bag, add chicken breast and remaining ingredients.
- Seal the bag of chicken mixture tightly and shake to coat well.

- Refrigerate to marinade for about 1 hour.
- Preheat the Outdoor Gas Griddle to medium-high heat.
- Grease the griddle. Generously
- Place the chicken breasts onto the griddle and cook for about 10 minutes per side.
- Serve hot.

Marinated Chicken Breast

(**Preparation time**: 1 hr 0 min | **Cook time**: 15 min | **Servings**: 1)

Ingredients:

- 12 Ounces (Boneless, Skinless) Chicken Breast Italian Dressing 5 Ounces

Instructions:

- Mix (In Ziplock bag) the chicken breast and Italian dressing.
- Poke holes in the bird with care.
- Refrigerate for at least 1-2 hour or up to 24 hours. Roate the chicken every now and again to evenly distribute the Italian dressing.
- Marinated chicken breast & preheat the Griddle to medium/low.
- Place the chicken breast on the griddle once it is heated. Any leftover marinade should be discarded.
- Cook until (5 minutes) the chicken is golden brown.
- Cook the Italian chicken breasts on the other side.
- When the chicken is almost done, use a digital thermometer to check the temperature. Cook the thickest part of the chicken until it reaches 165 degrees. Cooking the chicken over 165° will cause it to dry out and become tough.
- Remove the chicken from the griddle when it is fully done.

Chicken Wings with Sweet Red Chili and Peach Glaze

(**Preparation time:** 15 minutes | **Cooking time:** 30 minutes | **Servings:** 4)

Per serving: Calories: 195 Fat: 7 g Saturated Fat: 1 g Cholesterol: 60 mg Sodium: 182 mg

Carbs: 0 g Fiber: 0 g Sugar 0 g Protein: 31.6 g

Ingredients:

- 1 (12 oz.) jar peach preserves
- 1 cup sweet red chili sauce
- 1 teaspoon lime juice

- 1 tablespoon fresh cilantro, minced
- 1 (2-1/2 lb.) bag chicken wing sections
- Non-stick cooking spray

Instructions:

- Mix preserves, red chili sauce, lime juice and cilantro in a mixing bowl.
- Divide in half, and place one half aside for serving.
- Preheat griddle to medium heat and spray with non-stick cooking spray.
- Cook wings for 25 minutes turning several times until juices run clear.
- Remove wings from the griddle, toss in a bowl to coat wings with remaining glaze.
- Return wings to griddle and cook for an additional 3 to 5 minutes turning once.

Serve warm with your favorite dips and side dishes!

Chicken Phillies

(**Preparation time**: 10 min | **Cook time**: 15 min | **Servings**: 6)

Ingredients:

- 2 Tbsps vegetable oil
- 2 pounds of chicken breasts (thin strips)
- 2 onions thinly sliced
- 8 Ounces sliced mushrooms
- kosher salt, pepper, Old Bay seasoning
- 1 to 2 Tbsps worcestershire sauce
- 1/2 cup of sliced banana peppers
- 3 cloves garlic minced
- 6 hoagy/ sub buns
- 12 slices provolone cheese
- 1/2 cup of mayo

Instructions:

- Preheat the grill for several minutes on medium-high.
- Brush two sides of the grill with a tbsp of vegetable oil. Place the chicken on a side of the pan over the oil and the onions and mushrooms on the other.

- Using kosher salt, pepper, and Old Bay seasoning, season the chicken and onions/mushrooms. Cook for 6 to 8 minutes, rotating and turning a few times, then season both the chicken and the onions/mushrooms with worcestershire sauce.
- On the flat top grill, mix the chicken, onions, and mushrooms. Mix
- the banana peppers and garlic in a mixing bowl. Cook for another 6
- to 8 minutes, rotating and turning once or twice.
- To toast the buns, place them cut side down on the grill for a minute or two.
- Place 6 heaps of chicken and vegetables on the grill, top with 2 slices of provolone, and turn off the grill.
- Place the cheese on a bun with mayo after it has melted.

Teriyaki Chicken Stir Fry

(**Preparation time**: 5 min | **Cook time**: 10 min | **Total time**: 15 min)

Ingredients:

- Chicken Breast
- Favorite Veggies (fresh is obviously best, but stir fry blended veggies can be bought frozen)
- Teriyaki Sauce
- Extra Virgin Olive Oil
- White Rice (Optional, but a great addition)

Instructions:

- Begin by chopping the chicken breast into small pieces and placing it in a bowl.
- Place all of your chopped-up vegetables in a separate bowl.
- Prepare homemade teriyaki sauce or purchase a ready-to-use store-bought version.
- Preheat the Griddle to high, brush one side with oil and set the chicken on it.
- Cook for 2 minutes, flipping the chicken halfway through. On the opposite side of the griddle, spread the veggies and a little oil.
- Cook the chicken and veggies on separate grill surfaces until the chicken reaches an internal temperature of 165 degrees (turning regularly).
- Mix the chicken and vegetables on the grill after the chicken has reveryed the minimum internal temperature.
- Half of the teriyaki sauce is added first, then the remaining half is added, turning regularly. The Teriyaki Chicken Stir Fry is finished at this time. Remove the chicken and serve it over a bed of white rice or eat it plain.

Chicken Teriyaki

(Preparation time: 10 min | **Cook time:** 10 min | **Servings:** 4)

Ingredients:

- 1 1/2 pounds chicken thighs or chicken breasts (boneless & skinless) 4 cloves garlic minced
- 1/2 cup of teriyaki sauce
- 1 red bell pepper
- 1 yellow bell pepper
- 1 onion
- 8 oz mushrooms
- vegetable oil for the griddle
- kosher salt, pepper
- Optional: sesame seeds, green onions, more teriyaki sauce

Instructions:

- Cut the chicken into inch pieces and mix with the minced garlic and 1/4 cup of teriyaki sauce in a gallon plastic bag. Massage the bag until the contents are uniformly distributed. Refrigerate 1 hour or overnight.
- Bell peppers, onion, and mushrooms should all be thinly sliced.
- Set your Griddle to medium/medium-high heat and turn it on. On hot pan, add the chicken, vegetables, and the remaining 1/4 cup of teriyaki sauce. Season with kosher salt and pepper as needed.
- Cook for 7 to 9 minutes, tossing occasionally.
- If desired, top with sesame seeds, green onions, and extra teriyaki sauce.

Sizzling Chicken Fajitas

(Preparation time: 5 minutes | **Cooking time:** 25 minutes | **Servings:** 4)

Per serving: Calories: 398 Protein: 52 g Carbs: 20 g Fat: 18 g

Ingredients:

- 4 boneless chicken breast halves, thinly sliced
- 1 yellow onion, sliced
- 1 large green bell pepper, sliced
- 1 large red bell pepper, sliced
- 1 teaspoon ground cumin
- 1 teaspoon garlic powder

- 1 teaspoon onion powder
- 2 tablespoons lime juice
- 1 tablespoon olive oil
- 1/2 teaspoon black pepper
- 1 teaspoon salt
- 2 tablespoons vegetable oil
- 10 flour tortillas

Instructions:

- In a zipper-lock bag, combine the chicken, cumin, garlic, onion, lime juice, salt, pepper, and olive oil. Allow marinating for 30 minutes.
- Preheat griddle to medium heat.
- On one side of the griddle, add the olive oil and heat until shimmering.
- Add the onion and pepper and cook until slightly softened.
- On the other side of the griddle, add the marinated chicken and cook until lightly browned.
- Once the chicken is lightly browned, toss together with the onion and pepper and cook until the chicken registers 165°F.
- Remove chicken and vegetables from the griddle and serve with warm tortillas.

Hawaiian Chicken Skewers

(**Preparation time:** 70 minutes | **Cooking time:** 15 minutes | **Servings:** 4)

Per serving: Calories: 230 Protein: 28 g Carbs: 2 g Fat: 14 g

Ingredients:

- 3 lb. chicken breast, cut into 1 ½ inch cubes 2 cups pineapple, cut into 1 ½ inch cubes
- 2 large green peppers, cut into 1 ½ inch picces
- 1 large red onion, cut into 1 ½ inch pieces
- 2 tablespoons olive oil, to coat veggies For the marinade:
- 1/3 cup tomato paste
- 1/3 cup brown sugar, packed
- 1/3 cup soy sauce
- 1/4 cup pineapple juice
- 2 tablespoons olive oil
- 1 1/2 tablespoon mirin or rice wine vinegar
- 2 teaspoons garlic cloves, minced
- 1 tablespoon ginger, minced
- 1/2 teaspoon sesame oil

- Pinch of sea salt
- Pinch of ground black pepper
- 10 wooden skewers, for assembly

Instructions:

- Combine marinade ingredients in a mixing bowl until smooth. Reserve a 1/2 cup of the marinade in the refrigerator.
- Add chicken and remaining marinade to a sealable plastic bag and refrigerate for 1 hour.
- Preheat the griddle to medium heat.
- Add red onion, bell pepper, and pineapple to a mixing bowl with 2
- tablespoons olive oil and toss to coat.
- Thread chicken, red onion, pineapple, and bell pepper onto the skewers until all of the chicken has been used
- Place skewers on the griddle and grab your reserved marinade from the refrigerator; cook for 5 minutes, then brush with the remaining marinade and rotate.
- Brush again with marinade and sear for about 5 additional minutes or until chicken reads 165°F on a meat thermometer.
- Serve warm.

Fiery Italian Chicken Skewers

(**Preparation time:** 80 minutes | **Cooking time:** 20 minutes | **Servings:** 4)

Per serving: Calories: 945 Sodium: 798 mg Dietary Fiber: 3.2 g Fat: 46.7 g Carbs: 14.7 g Protein: 112.2 g

Ingredients:

- 10 chicken thighs, 1 red onion, cut into wedges
- 1 red pepperFor the marinade:
- 1/3 cup pine nuts
- 1 1/2 cups red peppers
- 2 Hot cherry peppers, stemmed and seeded, or to taste 1 cup packed fresh basil leaves, plus more to serve cloves garlic, peeled 1/4 cup grated Parmesan cheese
- 1 tablespoon paprika
- Extra virgin olive oil, as needed

Instructions:

- In a food processor or blender, add the toasted pine nuts, roasted red peppers, spicy cherry peppers, basil, garlic, Parmesan, and paprika. Process until well-combined.

- In order to use the pesto as a marinade for the chicken, add olive oil until the mixture becomes thin.
- Reserve half of the pesto for serving and transfer the other half to a big sealable plastic bag.
- Add the chicken thigh chunks to the bag of pesto, seal, and massage the bag to coat the chicken.
- Refrigerate for 1 hour.
- Preheat griddle to medium-high heat and brush with olive oil.
- Metal skewers are threaded with chicken cubes, red onion, and red pepper.
- Apply the saved pesto on the chicken.
- Cook for about 5 minutes on each side or until the chicken reaches an internal temperature of 165°F. Warm up and serve with your preferred salad or vegetables!

Chicken Thighs with Ginger-Sesame Glaze

(**Preparation time:** 10 minutes | **Cooking time:** 20 minutes | **Servings:** 4)

Per serving: Calories 266, Total fat 14g, Protein 33g, Carbs 2g

Ingredients:

- 8 boneless, skinless chicken thighs
- For the glaze:
- 3 tablespoons dark brown sugar
- 2 1/2 tablespoons soy sauce
- 1 tablespoon fresh garlic, minced
- 2 teaspoons sesame seeds
- 1 teaspoon fresh ginger, minced
- 1 teaspoon sambal oelek
- 1/3 cup scallions, thinly sliced
- Non-stick cooking spray

Instructions:

- Combine glaze ingredients in a large mixing bowl; separate and reserve half for serving.
- Add chicken to bowl and toss to coat well.
- Preheat the griddle to medium-high heat.
- Coat with cooking spray.
- Cook chicken for 6 minutes on each side or until done.
- Transfer chicken to plates and drizzle with remaining glaze to serve.

Buffalo Chicken Wings

(**Preparation time:** 10 minutes | **Cooking time:** 20 minutes | **Servings:** 8)

Per serving: Calories: 327 Fat: 19.8 g Saturated Fat: 3.6 g Cholesterol: 81 mg Sodium: 237 mg

Carbs: 1 g Fiber: 0.3 g Sugar: 0.2 g Protein: 36.1 g

Ingredients:

- 1 tablespoon sea salt
- 1 teaspoon ground black pepper
- 1 teaspoon garlic powder
- 2 lbs. chicken wings
- 2 tablespoons unsalted butter
- 1/3 cup buffalo sauce, like Moore's
- 1 tablespoon apple cider vinegar
- 1 tablespoon honey

Instructions:

- Toss the wings with the seasoning mixture to coat.
- Preheat griddle to medium heat.
- Place the wings on the griddle; make sure they are touching, so the meat stays moist on the bone while griddling.
- Flip wings every 5 minutes, for a total of 20 minutes of cooking.
- Heat the butter, buffalo sauce, vinegar and honey in a saucepan over low heat; whisk to combine well.
- Toss the wings with the sauce to coat.
- Turn griddle up to medium-high and place wings back on the griddle until the skins crisp, about 1 to 2 minutes per side.
- Add wings back into the bowl with the sauce and toss to serve.

Turkey Recipes

Cured Turkey Drumstick

(**Preparation time:** 10 minutes | **Cooking time:** 45 minutes | **Servings:** 3)

Per serving: Calories 266, Total fat 14g, Protein 33g, Carbs 2g

Ingredients:

- 3 fresh or thawed frozen turkey drumsticks
- 3 tablespoons of olive oil

For the brine

- 4 cups of filtered water
- ¼ cup of kosher salt, to taste
- ¼ cup of brown sugar
- 1 teaspoon of garlic powder
- 1 teaspoon of poultry seasoning
- ½ teaspoon of red pepper flakes
- 1 teaspoon of pink hardened salt

Instructions:

- Put the salt water ingredients in a 1-gallon sealable bag.
- Add the turkey drumstick to the salt water and refrigerate for 12 hours.
- After 12 hours, remove the drumstick from the saline, rinse with cold water, and pat dry with a paper towel.
- Air-dry the drumstick in the refrigerator without a cover for 2 hours.
- Remove the drumsticks from the refrigerator and rub a tablespoon of olive oil under and over each drumstick.
- Grease the cooking surface of the griddle with cooking spray.
- Turn on the 4 burners and turn their knobs to medium heat.
- Let the Griddle preheat for 5 minutes.
- Place the drumstick on the griddle and then let it cook for 20 minutes per side.
- Cook the turkey drumstick at 325°F until the internal temperature of the thickest part of each drumstick is 180°F with an instant reading digital thermometer.
- Place a smoked turkey drumstick under a loose foil tent for 15 minutes before eating.
- Serve.

Bourbon Turkey

(**Preparation time:** 15 minutes | **Cooking time:** 3 hours | **Servings:** 8)

Per serving: Calories 266, Total fat 14g, Protein 33g, Carbs 2g

Ingredients:

- 8 cups of chicken broth
- 1 stick of butter softened
- 1 teaspoon of thyme
- 1 (12 pounds) turkey
- 2 garlic cloves, minced
- 1 teaspoon of dried basil
- 1 teaspoon of pepper
- 1 teaspoon of salt
- 1 tablespoon of minced rosemary
- 1 teaspoon of paprika
- 1 lemon (wedged)
- 1 onion
- 1 apple (wedged)
- 1 orange (wedged)
- Maple bourbon glaze
- ¾ cup of bourbon
- ½ cup of maple syrup
- 1 stick of butter (melted)
- 1 tablespoon of lime

Instructions:

- Under cold running water, wash the turkey meat both inside and out.
- Place the lemon, onion, apple and orange in the cavity of the turkey.
- Combine the paprika, butter, thyme, basil, garlic, pepper, salt, and rosemary in a suitable mixing bowl.
-
- In a roasting pan, place a rack and the turkey on the rack.
- Grease the cooking surface of the griddle with cooking spray.
- Turn on the 4 burners and turn their knobs to medium heat.
- Let the Griddle preheat for 5 minutes.
- Cook for 1 hour on the griddle using the roasting pan with the cover on.
- In a suitable mixing bowl, combine all of the ingredients for the maple bourbon glaze. Mix until everything is well blended.

- Using a glaze mixture, baste the bird. Cove and smoke for another 2 hours, basting the turkey every 30 minutes and adding extra broth as needed, or until the internal temperature is 165°F.
- Serve.

Brine-Marinated Turkey Breast

(**Preparation time:** 15 minutes | **Cooking time:** 90 minutes | **Servings:** 6)

Per serving: Calories 266, Total fat 14g, Protein 33g, Carbs 2g

Ingredients:

For the brine

- 1 cup of kosher salt, to taste
- 1 cup of maple syrup
- ¼ cup of brown sugar
- ¼ cup of whole black peppercorns
- 4 cups of cold bourbon
- 1 ½ gallons of cold water
- 1 turkey breast of about 7 pounds

For turkey

- 3 tablespoons of brown sugar
- 1 ½ tablespoons of smoked paprika
- 1 ½ teaspoons of chipotle chili powder
- 1 ½ teaspoons of garlic powder
- 1 ½ teaspoons of salt, to taste
- 1 ½ teaspoons of black pepper, to taste
- 1 teaspoon of onion powder
- ½ teaspoon of ground cumin
- 6 tablespoons of melted unsalted butter

Instructions:

- Before beginning; make sure that the bourbon; the water, and the chicken stock are all cold
- Now to make the brine, combine the salt, the syrup, the sugar, the peppercorns, the bourbon, and the water in a large bucket altogether.
- Remove any pieces that are left on the turkey, like the neck or the giblets.
- Refrigerate the turkey meat in the brine for about 8 to 12 hours in a resealable bag.

- Remove the turkey breast then place it over a baking sheet and refrigerate for about 1 hour.
- Grease the cooking surface of the griddle with cooking spray.
- Turn on the 4 burners and turn their knobs to medium-low heat.
- Let the Griddle preheat for 5 minutes.
- In a suitable bowl, mix the paprika with the sugar, the chili powder, the garlic powder, the salt, the pepper, the onion powder and the cumin, mixing very
- well to combine.
- Carefully lift the skin of the turkey; then rub the melted butter over the meat Rub the spice over the meat very well and over the skin.
- Smoke the turkey breast for about 1 ½ hour at a temperature of about 375° F.
- Slice and serve.
- Serve.

Smoked Turkey Tabasco

(**Preparation time:** 15 minutes | **Cooking time:** 4 hours 45 minutes | **Servings:** 8)

Per serving: Calories 416; Fat 31g; Sodium 501mg; Carbs 16g; Fiber 2.1g; Sugar 2.2g; Protein 28g

Ingredients:

Ingredients:

- 1 Whole turkey (4-lbs.)

For the rub

- ¼ cup of brown sugar
- 2 teaspoons of smoked paprika
- 1 teaspoon of salt
- 1 ½ teaspoons of onion powder
- 2 teaspoons of oregano
- 2 teaspoons of garlic powder
- ½ teaspoon of dried thyme
- ½ teaspoon of white pepper
- ½ teaspoon of cayenne pepper, to taste

For the glaze

- ½ cup of ketchup
- ½ cup of hot sauce
- 1 tablespoon of cider vinegar

- 2 teaspoons of tabasco
- ½ teaspoon of Cajun spices
- 3 tablespoons of unsalted butter

Instructions:

- Rub the turkey with 2 tablespoons of brown sugar, smoked paprika, salt, onion powder, garlic powder, dried thyme, white pepper, and cayenne pepper. Let the turkey rest for an hour.
- Grease the cooking surface of the griddle with cooking spray.
- Turn on the 4 burners and turn their knobs to low heat.
- Let the Griddle preheat for 5 minutes.
- Place the seasoned turkey in the griddle and smoke for 4 hours.
- Place ketchup, hot sauce, cider vinegar, tabasco, and Cajun spices in a saucepan, then bring to a simmer.
- Remove the sauce from heat and quickly add unsalted butter to the saucepan.
- Stir until melted.
- After 4 hours of smoking, baste the tabasco sauce over the turkey, then continue smoking for 15 minutes.
- Serve.

Jalapeno Turkey in Broth

(**Preparation time:** 15 minutes | **Cooking time:** 3 hours 45 minutes | **Servings:** 4)

Per serving: Calories 318; Fat 15g; Sodium 521mg; Carbs 14g; Fiber 5.1g; Sugar 3g; Protein 27g

Ingredients:

- 5 pounds of the whole turkey, giblet removed
- ½ of the medium red onion, peeled and minced
- 8 jalapeño peppers
- 2 tablespoons of minced garlic
- 4 tablespoons of garlic powder
- 6 tablespoons of Italian seasoning
- 1 cup of butter, softened, unsalted
- ¼ cup of olive oil
- 1 cup of chicken broth

Instructions:

- Place a suitable saucepan over medium heat, add oil and butter, and when the butter melts, add onion, garlic, and peppers and then let it cook for 3 to 5
- minutes or until nicely golden brown.
- Pour in broth, stir well, let the mixture boil for 5 minutes, then remove the pan from the heat and strain the mixture to get just liquid.
- Inject turkey generously with prepared liquid, then spray the outside of turkey with butter spray and season well with garlic and Italian seasoning.
- Grease the cooking surface of the griddle with cooking spray.
- Turn on the 4 burners and turn their knobs to low heat.
- Let the Griddle preheat for 5 minutes.
- Place turkey on the griddle, shut with lid, and smoke for 30 minutes, then increase the temperature to medium-low and continue smoking the turkey for 3 hours.
- Serve.

Mayo Turkey

(**Preparation time:** 15 minutes | **Cooking time:** 4 hours 5 minutes | **Servings:** 10)

Per serving: Calories 401; Fat 13g; Sodium 161mg; Carbs 10g; Fiber 3.1g; Sugar 2g; Protein 25g

Ingredients:

- 1 Whole turkey (4-lbs., 1.8-kg.)
- For the rub
- ½ cup of mayonnaise
- Salt, to taste
- ¾ teaspoon of brown sugar
- ¼ cup of ground mustard
- 2 tablespoons of black pepper, to taste
- 1 teaspoon of onion powder
- 1 ½ tablespoons of ground cumin
- 1 ½ tablespoons of chili powder
- 2 tablespoons of cayenne pepper, to taste
- ½ tablespoon of old bay seasoning
- ½ teaspoon of the filling
- 3 cups of sliced green apples

Instructions:

- Place salt, brown sugar, brown mustard, black pepper, onion powder, ground cumin, chili powder, cayenne pepper, and old bay seasoning in a suitable bowl, then mix well. Set aside.
- Next, fill the turkey cavity with sliced green apples, then baste mayonnaise over the turkey skin.
- Sprinkle the dry spice mixture over the turkey, then wrap with aluminum foil.
- Marinate the turkey overnight and store it in the fridge to keep it fresh.
- On the next day, remove the turkey from the fridge and thaw at room temperature.
- Grease the cooking surface of the griddle with cooking spray.
- Turn on the 4 burners and turn their knobs to medium-low heat.
- Let the Griddle preheat for 5 minutes.
- Smoke the turkey for 4 hours or until the internal temperature has reached 170°F.
- Remove the smoked turkey from the griddle and serve.
- Serve.

Pork Recipes

Herb-rusted Mediterranean Pork Tenderloin

(Preparation time: 2 hours | **Cooking time:** 30 minutes | **Servings:** 4)

Ingredients:

- 1 pound pork tenderloin
- 1 tablespoon olive oil
- 2 teaspoons dried oregano
- 3/4 teaspoon lemon pepper
- 1 teaspoon garlic powder
- 1/4 cup parmesan cheese, grated
- 3 tablespoons olive tapenade

Instructions:

- Place pork on a large piece of plastic wrap.
- Rub tenderloin with oil, and sprinkle oregano, garlic powder, and lemon pepper evenly over the entire tenderloin.
- Refrigerate for 2 hours.
- Preheat griddle to medium-high heat.
- Transfer pork to a cutting board, remove the plastic wrap, and make a lengthwise cut through the center of the tenderloin, opening meat, so it lies flat, but do not cut all the way through.
- Combine tapenade and parmesan in a small mixing bowl; rub into the center of the tenderloin and fold meat back together.
- Tie together with twine in 2-inch intervals.
- Sear tenderloin for 20 minutes, turning tenderloin once during griddling, or until internal temperature reaches 145°F.
- Transfer tenderloin to cutting board.
- Tent with foil; let rest for 10 minutes.
- Remove string and cut into 1/4-inch-thick slices and serve.

Paprika Dijon Pork Tenderloin

(Preparation time: 10 minutes | **Cooking time:** 4 hours | **Servings:** 6)

Ingredients:

- 2 1 lb pork tenderloins

- 2 tablespoons Dijon mustard
- 1-1/2 teaspoons smoked paprika
- 1 teaspoon salt
- 2 tablespoons olive oil

Instructions:

- Place pork on a large piece of plastic wrap.
- In a small bowl, combine the mustard and paprika.
- Set your Griddle to medium heat.
- Rub the tenderloins with the mustard mixture, making sure they are evenly coated.
- Place the tenderloins on the Griddle and cook until all sides are well browned, and the internal temperature is 135°F.
- Remove the tenderloins from the Griddle and rest 5 minutes before slicing and serving.

Pork Ribs with Low-Sugar Ketchup

(**Preparation time**: 15 minutes | **Cook time**: 2 hrs | **Serves:** 6)

Per Serving: Calories 392; Fat 32g; Sodium 354mg; Carbs 14g; Fiber 1.2g; Sugar 5g; Protein 31g

Ingredients:

- 3 pounds country-style pork ribs
- 1 cup low-sugar ketchup
- ½ cup water
- ¼ cup onion, chopped
- ¼ cup cider vinegar or wine vinegar
- ¼ cup light molasses
- 2 tablespoons worcestershire sauce
- 2 teaspoons chili powder
- 2 garlic cloves, minced

Istructions:

- Mix the ketchup, water, onion, vinegar, molasses, worcestershire sauce, chili powder, and garlic in a saucepan Let this mixture to a boil then cook for 15
- minutes on a simmer with occasional stirring.
- Grease the cooking surface of the griddle with cooking spray.
- Turn on the 4 burners and turn their knobs to medium-low heat.

- Let the Griddle preheat for 5 minutes.
- Place ribs, bone-side down, on griddle and then let it cook for 1-½ to 2 hours, brushing occasionally with sauce.
- Serve with remaining sauce and enjoy!

Pork Chops with Pineapple and Bacon

(**Preparation time:** 15 minutes | **Cook time:** 60 minutes | **Serves:** 6)

Per Serving: Calories 339; Fat 13g; Sodium 421mg; Carbs 16g; Fiber 4.1g; Sugar 3.2g; Protein 27g

Ingredients:

- 1 large whole pineapple
- 6 pork chops
- 12 slices thick-cut bacon
- ¼ cup honey
- ⅛ teaspoon cayenne pepper, to taste

Istructions:

- Grease the cooking surface of the griddle with cooking spray.
- Turn on the 4 burners and turn their knobs to medium heat.
- Let the Griddle preheat for 5 minutes.
- Slice off the top and bottom of your pineapple, and peel the pineapple, cutting the skin off in strips.
- Cut pineapple flesh into 6 quarters.
- Wrap each pineapple section with a bacon slice; secure each end with a toothpick.
- Brush quarters with honey and sprinkle with cayenne pepper.
- Put the quarters on the griddle, flipping when bacon is cooked so that both sides are evenly griddleed.
- While pineapple quarters are cooking, coat pork chops with honey and cayenne pepper. Set on griddle.
- Tent with foil and then let it cook for 20 minutes.
- Flip, and continue cooking an additional 10 to 20 minutes or until chops are fully cooked.
- Serve each chop with a pineapple quarter on the side.

Baked Egg and Bacon-Stuffed Peppers

(**Preparation time:** 10 minutes | **Cooking time:** 15 minutes | **Servings:** 4 slices)

Ingredients:

- 1 cup shredded Cheddar cheese
- 4 slices bacon, cooked and chopped
- 4 bell peppers, seeded and tops removed
- 4 large eggs
- Sea salt
- Freshly ground black pepper
- Chopped fresh parsley, for garnish

Instructions:

- Preheat the Griddle to medium-high.
- Divide the cheese and bacon between the bell peppers. Put one of the eggs into each bell pepper, and season with salt and pepper.
- Place each bell pepper on the Griddle and cook for 13 minutes, until the egg are cooked and the yolks are slightly runny.
- Remove the peppers, garnish with parsley, and serve.

Sausage Mixed Grill

(**Preparation time:** 5 minutes | **Cooking time:** 22 minutes | **Servings:** 4 slices)

Ingredients:

- 8 mini bell peppers
- 2 heads radicchio cut into 6 wedges Canola oil, for brushing
- Sea salt
- Freshly ground black pepper
- 6 breakfast sausage links
- 6 hot or sweet Italian sausage links

Instructions:

- Preheat the Griddle to medium-high.
- Brush the bell peppers and radicchio with the oil. Season with salt and black pepper.
- Place the bell peppers and radicchio on the Griddle and cook for 10
- minutes without flipping.
- Meanwhile, poke the sausages with a fork or knife and brush them with some of the oil.

- After 10 minutes, remove the vegetables and set them aside. Decrease the heat to medium. Place the sausages on the Griddle and cook for 6
- minutes.
- Flip the sausages and cook for 6 minutes more. Remove the sausages from the Griddle

Cuban Pork Chops

(Preparation time: 30 minutes | **Cooking time:** 90 minutes | **Servings:** 4)

Ingredients:

- 4 pork chops
- 4 cloves garlic, smashed
- 2 tablespoons olive oil
- 1/3 cup lime juice
- 1/4 cup water
- 1 teaspoon ground cumin
- Salt and black pepper

Instructions:

- Set your Griddle to medium. Salt the pork chops on both sides and cook the chops until lightly browned.
- Combine the water, garlic, and lime juice in a bowl and whisk until even.
- Continue cooking the pork chops while basting them with the lime juice mixture.

Spicy Cajun Pork Chops

(Preparation time: 10 minutes | **Cooking time:** 90 minutes | **Servings:** 4)

Ingredients:

- 4 pork chops
- 1 tablespoon paprika
- 1/2 teaspoon ground cumin
- 1/2 teaspoon dried sage
- 1/2 teaspoon salt
- 1/2 teaspoon black pepper
- 1/2 teaspoon garlic powder
- 1/4 teaspoon cayenne pepper
- 1 tablespoon butter
- 1 tablespoon vegetable oil

Instructions:

- In a medium bowl, combine the paprika, cumin, sage, salt, pepper, garlic, and cayenne pepper.
- Heat your Griddle to medium-high heat and add the butter and oil.
- Rub the pork chops with an amount of the seasoning rub.
- Place the chops on the Griddle and cook for 4 to 5 minutes.
- Turn the pork chops and continue cooking for an additional 4 minutes.
- Remove the pork chops from the Griddle and allow to rest 5 minutes before serving.

Teriyaki-Marinated Pork Sirloin Tip Roast

(Preparation time: 45 minutes | **Cooking time:** 90 minutes | **Servings:** 4)

Ingredients:

- 1 (1½ to 2 pounds) pork sirloin tip roast
- Teriyaki marinade, for example, Mr. Yoshida's Original Gourmet Marinade

Instructions:

- Dry the roast with paper.
- Utilizing a 1-gallon cooler stockpiling sack or a sealable compartment, spread the roast with the teriyaki marinade.
- Refrigerate medium-term, turning at regular intervals.
- Cook the meat for 40 mins at 180°F.
- After 40 minutes, increase the temperature to 325°F.
- Cook the roast until the internal temperature, at the thickest part of the roast, arrives at 145°F.

Prime Rib of Pork

(Preparation time: 30 minutes | **Cooking time:** 3 hours | **Servings:** 6)

Ingredients:

- 1 (5-pound) rack of pork, around 6 ribs
- ¼ cup roasted garlic
- Extra-virgin olive oil
- 6 tablespoons Jan's Original Dry Rub, Pork Dry Rub, or your preferred pork roast rub

Instructions:

- Trim the cap and silver skin from the rack of pork. Remove the membrane from the bones by working a spoon handle under the bone membrane until you can get the membrane to pull it off.
- Rub the olive oil generously on all sides of the meat. Season with the rub, covering all sides of the meat. Double wrap the seasoned rack of pork in plastic wrap and refrigerate for 2 to 4 hours or medium-term.
- Remove the seasoned rack of pork from the refrigerator and let sit at room temperature for 30 minutes before cooking. Preheat the Griddle to 225°F.
- Place the rack rib-side down directly on the Griddle.
- Cook the rack of pork for 1 to 1½ hours until the internal temperature arrives at 140°F.
- Remove the meat from the Griddle, and let it rest under a free foil tent for 15 minutes before cutting.

Tender Griddle Loin Chops

(**Preparation time:** 10 minutes | **Cooking time:** 13 minutes | **Servings:** 6)

Ingredients:

- 6 boneless focus cut midsection pork cleaves
- 1 to 1½ inches thick 2 quarts Pork Brine
- 2 tablespoons roasted garlic–seasoned extra-virgin olive oil
- 2 teaspoons black pepper

Instructions:

- Trim abundance fat and silver skin from the pork slashes.
- Place the pork slashes and brine in a 1-gallon sealable pack and refrigerate for in any event 12 hours or medium-term.
- Remove the pork slashes from the brine and pat them dry with paper towels.
- Brined pork hacks cook quicker than un-brined cleaves, so be mindful so as to screen internal temperatures.
- Rest the pork slashes under a foil tent for 5 minutes before serving.

Florentine Ribeye Pork Loin

(**Preparation time:** 30 minutes | **Cooking time:** 70 minutes | **Servings:** 7)

Ingredients:

- 1 (3-pound) boneless ribeye pork loin roast
- 4 tablespoons extra-virgin olive oil, divided
- 2 tablespoons Pork Dry Rub or your favorite pork seasoning 4 bacon slices
- 6 cups fresh spinach
- 1 small red onion, diced
- 6 cloves garlic, cut into thin slivers
- ¾ cup shredded mozzarella cheese

Instructions:

- Trim away any abundance of fat and silver skin.
- Butterfly the pork loin or approach your butcher to butterfly it for you.
- There are numerous phenomenal recordings online with nitty-gritty directions on the various systems for butterflying a loin roast.
- Rub 2 tablespoons of the olive oil on each side of the butterflied roast
- and season the two sides with the rub.
- Cook the bacon in a large griddle over medium heat. Disintegrate and set aside. Reserve the bacon fat.
- Griddle the pork loin for 60 to 75 minutes, or until the internal temperature at the thickest part arrives at 140°F.
- Rest the pork loin under a free foil tent for 15 minutes before cutting, contrary to what would be expected.

Beef Recipes

Grilled Flat Iron

(**Preparation time:** 10 minutes | **Cooking time:** 15 minutes | **Servings:** 2)

Ingredients:

- 1 ½ lb. flat iron steak
- Doreen's Steak Marinade
- Olive oil, for greasing, as needed

Instructions:

- Add the steak in the resealable bag with the Doreen's Steak Marinade, seal it, and then knead until thoroughly mixed.
- Keep in your fridge, then let it marinade for 2 hours or overnight if desired.
- Warm your gas griddle to high heat, then grease with olive oil.
- Putt of the steak from the bag and shake off excess marinade. Cook the flat iron steaks on the gas grill until your desired doneness is achieved. Slice before serving.

Sweet e Spicy Teriyaki Beef Kebabs

(**Preparation time:** 10 minutes | **Cooking time:** 8 minutes | **Servings:** 4)

Ingredients:

- 1 lb. beef strip steak, cut into cubes
- Spicy Orange Teriyaki Marinade, as needed
- Olive oil, for greasing, as needed

Instructions:

- Add the steak cubes to the Spicy Orange Teriyaki Marinade. Knead to coat well. Keep in your refrigerator for 30 minutes to 8 hours if desired. Warm the gas griddle to high heat and grease with olive oil.
- Remove the steak cubes from the Spicy Orange Teriyaki Marinade, then thread it onto skewers.
- Put the skewers on your hot gas griddle, then cook for 8 minutes, flipping every 2 minutes for all sides to cook evenly. Remove, then serve.

Herb-Marinated Steak Tips

(**Preparation time:** 10 minutes | **Cooking time:** 10 minutes | **Servings:** 4)

Ingredients:

- 1 lb. top sirloin steak, cut into cubes
- Herb Steak Marinade

Instructions:

- Put the top sirloin steak cubes into a bag filled with Herb Steak Marinade, seal, and knead to mix evenly. Keep in your fridge overnight to marinate.
- Warm the gas griddle to high heat and grease with olive oil. Remove the meat from the Herb Steak Marinade bag, shaking off excess marinade before cooking.
- Put steak cubes onto your gas griddle, then cook for 5 minutes or until evenly grilled.

Butte Montana- Style Beef Pasty

(**Preparation time:** 20 minutes | **Cooking time:** 15 minutes | **Servings:** 4)

Ingredients:

- 16 oz. top sirloin, sliced into cubes
- 2 cups potato, cubed & cooked
- All-In Meat Seasoning (see my recipe here)
- 1 tbsp. Dijon mustard (optional)
- 2 tbsp. oil
- 1 package of 2 piecrust rolls
- 1 egg, plus 1 tbsp. water

Instructions:

- Flavor the beef with the All-In Meat Seasoning, mustard (if using), and oil in a large bowl. Mix to combine well, then keep it in your refrigerator for 30
- minutes or overnight. Warm your gas griddle to medium-high and your air fryer to 350°F.
- Cook the beef, stirring often, for 3–5 minutes or until the cubes are slightly pink in the center. Keep it aside to cool. Once the beef is cooled, fold them in the potato cubes until thoroughly mixed. Unroll your piecrust, then lay it on your clean work surface.
- Add ½ of the beef and potato batter on the left side of the pie crust, orming a half-moon shape. Repeat the process with the other ½ of the batter. Leave a 1-inch gap in the center and all around the sides.
- Add another crust sheet over the beef-potato mixture, pressing it first down the middle to divide. Press the piecrust on all side edges to seal. Slice the middle part of the piecrust to separate the 2 pockets, pressing the open side again to seal.
- Whisk the egg and 1 tbsp. of water to make egg wash in a small bowl.
- Brush the egg wash mixture on top and on all sides of the pasty.

- Transfer the pasty on a piece of parchment paper and into the air fryer. Air fry for 15 minutes or until golden brown. Serve.

Sear Ribeye with Smoked Garlic e Vegetables

(**Preparation time:** 15 minutes | **Cooking time:** 37 minutes | **Servings:** 2)

Ingredients:

- 1 ½ lb. ribeye steak, boneless
- 6–10 large garlic cloves
- Steak Dry Rub, as needed
- 2 tbsp. unsalted butter
- 2 zucchinis, sliced
- ½ red bell pepper, cut in strips
- 1 white onion, cut in half
- 2 Portobello mushrooms
- 1 cup applewood chips
- Olive oil, as needed
- Herb Salt, as needed, (optional)

Instructions:

- Put an aluminum tray on your resting rack. Add the wood chips into the aluminum tray, then light using a torch. Blow out the fire to make a smoke once the wood chips are burning. Add the ribeye steak and garlic to the tray.
- Cover the entire resting rack with a dome. Let the meat and garlic smoke for 20–30 minutes. Warm your gas griddle to medium-high heat, then grease with olive oil.
- Flavor the ribeye steak generously with Steak Dry Rub, then put into the smoking olive oil. Cook for 2–3 minutes, flipping it as often as you like to sear all sides. Before the cooking time is complete, add the garlic in the olive oil and let it slightly caramelize.
- Transfer the garlic to the cooler side of your gas griddle, add the rosemary, then pour a bit of water on top, covering it with a dome to finish cooking.
- Remove the cooked steak, then let it rest for 5 mins.
- Add the fresh butter to the beef fat on the hot side of your gas griddle, then add your vegetables. If desired, season it with Herb Salt, then cook for 2
- minutes on each side.
- Before serving, slice the steak, then put it over the veggies, and garnish it with the garlic on the top. Serve.

Seared Garlic Ribeye with Carrots, Asparagus e Gremolata

(**Preparation time:** 15 minutes | **Cooking time:** 17 minutes | **Servings:** 2)

Ingredients:

- 4 8–10 oz. Ribeye steaks
- 6–8 cherry tomatoes, sliced into half lengthwise A handful of asparagus, cleaned & trimmed
- 6 – 8 large garlic cloves
- Olive oil, as needed
- Rib Seasoning Blend, as required
- For the Gremolata:
- ½ cup parsley, chopped
- 3 tbsp. lemon juice
- 3 tbsp. Olive oil
- 2 tsp. lemon zest
- 1 tsp. garlic, grated
- Herb Salt, to taste
- Ground black pepper, to taste

Instructions:

- Warm your gas griddle to medium-high heat, then pour 1–2 tbsp. olive oil to grease. Add the tomatoes, cut lengthwise, and cook for 2–3 minutes. Set aside.
- Flavor the steaks on both sides with Rib Seasoning Blend, then put it on the gas griddle. Cook for 3–4 mins on every side or until evenly cooked.
- On the first flip, add the garlic cloves and asparagus with a bit of Herb Salt and pepper and cook for 4–5 mins, stirring it often.
- Mix all the Gremolata ingredients in a bowl evenly, then set it aside.
- Remove the cooked steak from your gas griddle and let it rest for 4–5
- minutes.
- Before serving, put the tomatoes and asparagus on your serving plate, then top it with the ribeye steak. Spoon the Gremolata and the caramelized garlic on top. Serve and enjoy.

Garlicky Sirloin Beef with Parmesan

(**Preparation time:** 15 minutes| **Cook time:** 10 minutes| **Serves:**8)

Per Serving: Calories 542; Fat 27.1g; Sodium 225mg; Carbs 1.6g; Fiber 0.6g; Sugar 0.1g; Protein 65.8g

Ingredients:

- 4-pound Sirloin Beef, Cut into 1-Inch Cubes
- 12 Garlic Cloves, Finely Minced
- ½ Cup Olive Oil
- Sea Salt to Taste
- ½ Cup Grated Parmesan

Istructions:

- Combine the ingredients in a closed bowl or bag and store in the refrigerator for 3 hours to overnight.
- Using skewers, attach the meat chunks to the skewers.
- Preheat the Griddle to high heat and cook the chicken for 3 minutes per side, sprinkle each side with parmesan cheese.
- Grill for a few minutes longer, or until it's done to your liking.
- Formerly portion, let the meat to rest for a few minutes.
- Cook the remaining half of the ingredients with the same steps.
- Serve and enjoy.

Juicy NY Strip Steak Griddle

(**Preparation time:** 45 minutes | **Cooking time:** 8 minutes | **Servings:** 1)

Ingredients:

- (8 ounce) NY strip steak
- Olive oil
- Sea salt
- Fresh ground black pepper

Instructions:

- Putt off the steak from the fridge and let it come to room temperature, about 30 to 45 minutes.
- Preheat griddle to medium-high heat and brush with olive oil, season the steak on all sides with salt and pepper. Cook steak about 4 to 5 minutes.
- Flip and cook about 4 minutes more for medium rare steak; between 125°F
- and 130°F on a meat thermometer.
- Transfer the steak to a plate and rest it for 5 minutes before serving.

Lamb Recipes

Grilled Lamb Burgers

(**Preparation time:** 10 minutes | **Cooking time:** 20 minutes | **Servings:** 5)

Ingredients:

- 1 ¼ lb. ground lamb
- 1 egg
- 1 tsp. dried oregano
- 1 tsp. dry sherry
- 1 tsp. white wine vinegar
- 4 garlic cloves, minced
- Red pepper to taste
- ½ cup chopped green onions
- 1 tbsp. chopped mint
- 2 tbsp. chopped cilantro
- 2 tbsp. dry breadcrumbs
- 1/8 tsp. salt to taste
- ¼ tsp. ground black pepper
- 5 hamburger buns

Instructions:

- Preheat a griddle to 350–450°F then grease its grates.
- Using a large mixing bowl, add in all the ingredients on the list except the buns then mix properly to combine with clean hands.
- Make about five patties out of the mixture then set aside.
- Place the lamb patties on the preheated grill and cook for about 7 to 9
- minutes turning only once until an inserted thermometer reads 160°F.
- Serve the lamb burgers on the hamburger buns, add your favorite
- toppings, and enjoy.

Lamb Shank

(**Preparation time:** 10 minutes | **Cooking time:** 4 hours | **Servings:** 6)

Ingredients:

- 8-oz. red wine
- 2-oz. whiskey

- 2 tbsp. minced fresh rosemary
- 1 tbsp. minced garlic
- Black pepper to taste
- 6 (1 ¼-lb.) lamb shanks

Ingredients:

- Add all ingredients except the lamb shank and mix till well combined.
- In a large resealable bag, add the marinade and lamb shank.
- Seal the bag and shake completely.
- Refrigerate for about 24 hours.
- Preheat the Griddle to 225°F.
- Arrange the leg of lamb in the Griddle and cook for about 4 hours.

Lamb Skewers

(**Preparation time:** 5 minutes | **Cooking time:** 10 minutes | **Servings:** 6)

Ingredients:

- 1 lemon, juiced
- 2 garlic cloves, crushed
- 2 red onions, chopped
- 1 tbsp. thyme, chopped
- Salt and pepper to taste
- 1 tsp. oregano
- 1/3 cup oil
- ½ tsp. cumin
- 2 lb. cubed lamb leg

Instructions:

- Refrigerate the chunked lamb.
- The remaining ingredients should be mixed. Add in the meat.
- Refrigerate overnight.
- Pat the meat dry and thread onto some metal or wooden skewers.
- Wooden skewers should be soaked in water.
- Preheat your Griddle, with your lid closed, until it reaches 450°F.
- Grill, covered, for 4–6 minutes on each side.
- Serve.

Lamb Ribs Rack

(**Preparation time:** 10 minutes | **Cooking time:** 2 hours | **Servings:** 2)

Ingredients:

- 2 tbsp. fresh sage
- 2 tbsp. fresh rosemary
- 2 tbsp. fresh thyme
- 2 peeled garlic cloves
- 1 tbsp. honey
- Black pepper to taste
- ¼ cup olive oil
- 1 (1 ½-lb.) trimmed rack lamb ribs.

Instructions:

- Combine all ingredients in a blender.
- Slowly add oil and pulse till a smooth paste is formed.
- Coat the rib rack with paste generously and refrigerate for about 2
- hours.
- Preheat the Griddle to 225°F.
- Arrange the rib rack in the Griddle and cook for about 2 hours.
- Remove the rib rack from the Griddle and transfer onto a cutting board for about 10–15 minutes before slicing.
- With a sharp knife, cut the rib rack into equal-sized individual ribs and serve

Lamb Chops

(**Preparation time:** 10 minutes | **Cooking time:** 12 minutes | **Servings:** 6)

Ingredients:

- 6 (6-oz.) lamb chops
- 3 tbsp. olive oil
- Salt and ground black pepper to taste

Instructions:

- Preheat the Griddle to 450°F.
- Coat the lamb with oil and season with salt and black pepper evenly.
- Arrange the chops in the griddle grate and cook for about 4–6 minutes per side.

Cocoa Crusted Grilled Flank Steak

(**Preparation time:** 15 minutes | **Cooking time:** 6 minutes | **Servings:** 7)

Ingredients:

- 1 tbsp. cocoa powder
- 2 tbsp. chili powder
- 1 tbsp. chipotle chili powder
- ½ tbsp. garlic powder
- ½ tbsp. onion powder
- 1-1/2 tbsp. brown sugar
- 1 tbsp. cumin
- 1 tbsp. smoked paprika
- 1 tbsp. kosher salt
- ½ tbsp. black pepper
- 1 tbsp. olive oil
- 4 lb. Flank steak

Instructions:

- Whisk together cocoa, chili powder, chipotle, garlic powder, onion powder, sugar, cumin, paprika, salt, and pepper in a mixing bowl.
- Drizzle the steak with oil, then rub with the cocoa mixture on both sides.
- Preheat your Griddle for 15 minutes with the lid closed.
- Cook the meat on the grill grate for 5 minutes or until the internal temperature reaches 135°F.
- Remove the meat from the grill and cool for 15 minutes to allow the juices to redistribute.
- Slice the meat against the grain and on a sharp diagonal.
- Serve and enjoy.

Bone In-Turkey Breast

(**Preparation time:** 20 minutes | **Cooking time:** 2 hours | **Servings:** 7)

Ingredients:

- 1 (8–10 lbs.) boned turkey breast
- 6 tbsp. extra-virgin olive oil
- 5 Yang original dry lab or poultry seasonings

Instructions:

- Configure a griddle for indirect cooking and preheat to 225°F.
- Add oil and seasonings to the turkey and place it on the Griddle.
- Smoke the boned turkey breast directly in a V rack or grill at 225°F for 2 hours.
- After 2 hours of hickory smoke, raise the pit temperature to 325°F.

- Roast until the turkey breast reaches an internal temperature of 170°F and the juice is clear.
- Place the hickory-smoked turkey breast under a loose foil tent for 20
- minutes, then scrape the grain.

Grilled Lamb Sandwiches

(**Preparation time:** 5 minutes | **Cooking time:** 40 minutes | **Servings:** 6)

Ingredients:

- 1 (4 lbs.) boneless lamb
- 1 cup raspberry vinegar
- 2 tbsp. olive oil
- 1 tbsp. chopped fresh thyme
- 2 pressed garlic cloves
- ¼ tsp. salt to taste
- ¼ tsp. ground pepper
- 1 sliced bread

Instructions:

- Using a large mixing bowl, add in the raspberry vinegar, oil, thyme, and garlic, then mix properly to combine. Add in the lamb, toss to combine then let it sit in the refrigerator for about 8 hours or overnight.
- Next, discard the marinade and season the lamb with salt and pepper to taste. Preheat a griddle and grill to 400–500°F, add in the seasoned lamb, and grill for about 30 to 40 minutes until it attains a temperature of 150°F.
- Once cooked, let the lamb cool for a few minutes, slice as desired then serve on the bread with your favorite topping.

Yan's Grilled Quarters

(**Preparation time:** 20 minutes | **Cooking time:** 90 minutes | **Servings:** 4)

Ingredients:

- 4 fresh or thawed frozen chicken quarters
- 4–6 glasses extra-virgin olive
- 4 tbsp. Yang original dry lab

Instructions:

- Configure a griddle for indirect cooking to preheat to 325°F.
- Add oil and seasoning to the chicken.

- Place chicken on the grill and cook at 325°F for 1 hour.
- After one hour, raise the pit temperature to 400°F to finish the chicken and crisp the skin.
- When the temperature of the part of the thighs and feet reaches 180°F and the juice becomes clear, pull the crispy chicken out of the grill.
- Let the crispy grilled chicken rest under a loose foil tent for 15 minutes before eating.

Fish and Seafood Recipes

Grilled King Crab Legs

(**Preparation time:** 10 minutes | **Cooking time:** 25 minutes | **Servings:** 4)

Ingredients:

- 4 lbs. king crab legs (split)
- 4 tbsp lemon juice
- 2 tbsp garlic powder
- 1 cup butter (melted)
- 2 tsp brown sugar
- 2 tsp paprika
- Black pepper (depends on your liking)

Instructions:

- In a mixing bowl, combine the lemon juice, butter, sugar, garlic, paprika and pepper.
- Arrange the split crab on a baking sheet, split side up.
- Drizzle ¾ of the butter mixture over the crab legs.
- Configure your Griddle for indirect cooking and preheat it to 225°F, 5. Arrange the crab legs onto the griddle grate, shell side down.
- Cover the Griddle and cook for 25 minutes.
- Remove the crab legs from the Griddle.
- Serve and top with the remaining butter mixture.

Cajun Smoked Catfish

(**Preparation time:** 15 minutes | **Cooking time:** 2 hours | **Servings:** 4)

Ingredients:

- 4 catfish fillets (5 oz each)
- ½ cup Cajun seasoning
- 1 tsp ground black pepper
- 1 tbsp smoked paprika
- ¼ tsp cayenne pepper
- 1 tsp hot sauce
- 1 tsp granulated garlic
- 1 tsp onion powder

- 1 tsp thyme & 1 tsp salt or more to taste 2 tbsp chopped fresh parsley

Instructions:

- Pour water into the bottom of a square or rectangular dish. Add 4 tbsp salt. Arrange the catfish fillets into the dish. Cover the dish and refrigerate for 3 to 4 hours.
- Combine the paprika, cayenne, hot sauce, onion, salt, thyme, garlic, pepper and Cajun seasoning in a mixing bowl.
- Remove the fish from the dish and let it sit for a few minutes, or until it is at room temperature. Dry the fish with a paper towel.
- Rub the seasoning mixture over each fillet generously.
- Start your Griddle on smoke, leaving the lid open for 5 minutes, or until fire starts.
- Keep lid unopened and preheat to 200°F,
- Arrange the fish fillets onto the griddle grate and close the Griddle.
- Cook for about 2 hours, or until the fish is flaky.
- Remove the fillets from the Griddle and let the fillets rest for a few minutes to cool.
- Serve and garnish with chopped fresh parsley.

Grilled Tilapia

(**Preparation time:** 10 minutes | **Cooking time:** 20 minutes| **Servings:** 6)

Ingredients:

- 2 tsp dried parsley
- ½ tsp garlic powder
- 1 tsp cayenne pepper
- ½ tsp ground black pepper
- ½ tsp thyme
- ½ tsp dried basil
- ½ tsp oregano
- 3 tbsp olive oil
- ½ tsp lemon pepper
- 1 tsp kosher salt
- 1 lemon (juiced)
- 6 tilapia fillets
- 1 ½ tsp creole seafood seasoning

Instructions:

- In a mixing bowl, combine spices
- Brush the fillets with oil and lemon juice.
- Liberally, season all sides of the tilapia fillets with the seasoning mix.

- Preheat your Griddle to 325°F
- Place a non-stick BBQ griddle try on the Griddle and arrange the tilapia fillets onto it.
- Griddle for 15 to 20 minutes
- Remove fillets and cool down

Salmon with Togarashi

(**Preparation time:** 5 minutes | **Cooking time:** 20 minutes| **Servings:** 3)

Ingredients:

- 1 salmon fillet
- ¼ cup olive oil
- ½ tbsp kosher salt
- 1 tbsp Togarashi seasoning

Instructions:

- Preheat your Griddle to 400°F.
- Place the salmon on a sheet lined with non-stick foil with the skin side down.
- Rub the oil into the meat, then sprinkle salt and Togarashi.
- Place the salmon on the Griddle and cook for 20 minutes or until the internal temperature reaches 145oF with the lid closed.
- Remove from the Griddle and serve when hot.

Crab stuffed Lingcod

(**Preparation time:** 20 minutes | **Cooking time:** 30 minutes| **Servings:** 6)

Ingredients:

Lemon cream sauce:

- 4 garlic cloves
- 1 shallot
- 1 leek
- 2 tbsp olive oil
- 1 tbsp salt
- ¼ tbsp black pepper
- 3 tbsp butter
- ¼ cup white wine

- 1 cup whipping cream
- 2 tbsp lemon juice
- 1 tbsp lemon zest

Crab mix:

- 1 lb. crab meat
- ⅓ cup mayo
- ⅓ cup sour cream
- ⅓ cup lemon cream sauce
- ¼ green onion, chopped
- ¼ tbsp black pepper
- ½ tbsp old bay seasoning

Fish:

- 2 lb. lingcod
- 1 tbsp olive oil
- 1 tbsp salt
- 1 tbsp paprika
- 1 tbsp green onion, chopped
- 1 tbsp Italian parsley

Instructions:

Lemon cream sauce:

- Chop garlic, shallot, and leeks, then add to a saucepan with oil, salt, pepper, and butter.
- Sauté over medium heat.
- Deglaze with white wine, then add whipping cream. Bring the sauce to boil, reduce heat, and simmer for 3 minutes.
- Add lemon juice and lemon zest. Blend the souce until smooth.
- Set aside ⅓ cup for the crab mix

Crab mix:

- Add all the fixings to a mixing bowl and mix thoroughly until well combined.
- Set aside

Fish:

- Fire up your Griddle to high heat, then slice the fish into 6-oz portions.
- Lay the fish on its side on a cutting board and slice it ¾ way through the middle leaving a ½ inch on each end to have a nice pouch.

- Rub the oil into the fish, then place them on a baking sheet. Sprinkle with salt.
- Stuff crab mix into each fish, then sprinkle paprika and place it on the Griddle.
- Cook for 15 minutes or more if the fillets are more than 2 inches thick.
- Remove the fish and transfer them to serving platters. Pour the remaining lemon cream sauce on each fish and garnish with onions and parsley.

Smoked Shrimp

(Preparation time: 10 minutes | **Cooking time:** 10 minutes| **Servings:** 6)

Ingredients:

- 1 lb. tail-on shrimp, uncooked
- ½ tbsp onion powder
- ½ tbsp garlic powder
- ½ tbsp salt
- 4 tbsp teriyaki sauce
- 2 tbsp green onion, minced
- 4 tbsp sriracha mayo

Instructions:

- Peel the shrimp shells leaving the tail on, then wash well and rise.
- Pat dry with a paper towel.
- Preheat your Griddle to 450°F.
- Season the shrimp with onion powder, garlic powder, and salt. Place the shrimp on the Griddle and cook for 6 minutes on each side.
- Remove the shrimp from the Griddle and toss with teriyaki sauce, then garnish with onions and mayo.

Salmon Fillets with Basil Butter e Broccolini

(Preparation time: 10 minutes | **Cooking time:** 12 minutes| **Servings:** 2)

Ingredients:

- 2 (6-oz) salmon fillets, skin removed
- 2 tbsp butter, unsalted
- 2 basil leaves, minced
- 1 garlic clove, minced
- 6 oz broccolini
- 2 tsp olive oil

- Sea salt, to taste

Instructions:

- Garlic, basil, and butter should all be thoroughly combined. When ready to serve, shape into a ball and store in the fridge.
- Preheat the Griddle to medium-high heat.
- Season the salmon fillet with salt.
- Add broccolini, salt, and olive oil to a bowl, toss to coat and set aside.
- Brush griddle with olive oil, and cook salmon, skin side down, for 12minutes. Turn on the salmon and cook for 4 minutes.
- Allow to rest while the broccolini cooks.
- Add the broccolini to the Griddle, turning occasionally, until slightly charred, about 6 minutes.
- Top each salmon fillet with a slice of basil butter and Servings with a side of broccolini.

Spiced Snapper with Mango and Red Onion Salad

(Preparation time: 10 minutes | **Cooking time:** 20 minutes| **Servings:** 4)

Ingredients:

- 2 red snappers, cleaned
- Sea salt
- ⅓ cup tandoori spice
- Olive oil, plus more for Griddle
- Extra-virgin olive oil, for drizzling
- Lime wedges, for serving

For the salsa:

- 1 ripe of firm mango, peeled and chopped
- 1 small red onion, thinly sliced
- 1 bunch of cilantro, coarsely chopped
- 3 tbsp fresh lime juice

Instructions:

- Combine the mango, onion, cilantro, lime juice, and a generous amount of salt. Drizzle in a olive oil and toss once more to coat.
- Place snapper on a cutting board and pat dry with paper towels. Cut slashes crosswise on a diagonal along the body every 2" on both sides, cutting down to the bones.
- Season fish inside and out with salt. Coat fish with tandoori spice.

- Preheat the Griddle to medium-high heat and brush with oil.
- Griddle fish for 10 minutes, undisturbed, until skin is puffed and charred.
- Flip and griddle fish until the other side is lightly charred and the skin is puffed for about 8 to 12 minutes.
- Transfer to a platter.
- Top with mango salad and Servings with lime wedges.

Spiced Salmon

(Preparation time: 10 minutes | **Cooking time:** 8 minutes | **Servings:** 6)

Ingredients:

- ½ tablespoon ground ginger
- ½ tablespoon ground coriander
- ½ tablespoon ground cumin
- ½ teaspoon paprika
- ¼ teaspoon cayenne pepper
- Salt, as required
- 1 tablespoon fresh orange juice
- 1 tablespoon coconut oil, melted
- 2 pounds salmon fillets

Instructions:

- In a bowl, add spices, salt, orange juice and oil and mix until a paste forms.
- Add salmon fillets and coat with mixture generously.
- Refrigerate to marinate for about 30 minutes.
- Preheat the Outdoor Gas Griddle to high heat.
- Grease the griddle.
- Place the salmon fillets onto the griddle, skin-side down and cover with the cooking dome.
- Cook for about 3-4 minutes per side.
- Serve hot.

Glazed Salmon

(Preparation time: 15 minutes | **Cooking time:** 36 minutes | **Servings:** 4)

Ingredients:

- 1/3 cup low-sodium soy sauce

- 1/3 cup fresh orange juice
- ¼ cup maple syrup
- 1 scallion, chopped
- 1 teaspoon garlic powder
- 1 teaspoon ground ginger
- 1 (1½ pound) salmon fillet

Instructions:

For marinade:

- In a bowl, add all ingredients except for salmon and mix well.
- In a shallow bowl, add salmon and 2/3 cup of marinade and mix well.
- Refrigerate to marinate for about 1 hour, flipping occasionally.
- Reserve the remaining marinade.
- Preheat the Outdoor Gas Griddle to medium heat.
- Grease the griddle.
- Place the salmon fillets onto griddle, skin-side down and cover with the cooking dome.
- Cook for about 15-18 minutes per side.
- In the final 5 minutes of cooking, coat the salmon fillet with reserved marinade.
- Remove the salmon fillet from griddle and place onto a cutting board.
- Cut the salmon into desired-sized fillets and serve.

Sweet e Sour Salmon

(**Preparation time:** 15 minutes | **Cooking time:** 38 minutes| **Servings:** 4)

Ingredients:

- 4 teaspoons olive oil, divided
- ¼ cup dark brown sugar
- ¼ cup pineapple juice
- 2 tablespoons fresh lemon juice
- 2 tablespoons white vinegar
- ½ teaspoon paprika
- ½ teaspoon cayenne pepper
- ¼ teaspoon garlic powder
- Salt and ground black pepper, as required
- 4 (5-ounce) salmon fillets

Instructions:

- In a saucepan, add 2 teaspoons of oil and remaining ingredients except for salmon fillets and stir to combine.
- Place the saucepan of oil mixture over medium-low heat and bring to a boil, stirring occasionally.
- Now adjust the heat to low and simmer, uncovered for about 15
- minutes, stirring occasionally.
- Preheat the Outdoor Gas Griddle to medium heat.
- Grease the griddle.
- Rub the salmon fillets with remaining olive oil and then sprinkle with salt and black.
- Place the salmon fillets onto griddle and cook for about 3-4 minutes per side.
- Remove the salmon fillets from griddle and brush each fillet with the honey sauce.
- Serve hot.

Cod Parcel

(**Preparation time:** 10 minutes | **Cooking time:** 24 minutes| **Servings:** 4)

Ingredients:

- 4 (4-ounce) cod fillets
- ¼ cup fresh lemon juice
- 2 tablespoons coconut oil, melted
- 2 tablespoons fresh rosemary, chopped
- Salt and ground black pepper, as required 1 onion, slice thinly

Instructions:

- Preheat the Outdoor Gas Griddle to medium-high heat.
- Arrange 4 square pieces of foil onto a smooth surface.
- Place 1 cod fillet over each foil square.
- In a bowl, blend together lemon juice, coconut oil, rosemary, salt and black pepper.
- Pour parsley mixture evenly over cod fillets.
- Arrange onion slices
- Fold the foil around cod mixture to seal it.
- Place the cod parcels onto the griddle and cook for about 5-7 minutes per side.

Spiced Whole Trout

(**Preparation time:** 10 minutes | **Cooking time:** 20 minutes| **Servings:** 2)

Ingredients:

- 1 teaspoon vegetable oil

- 2 teaspoons fresh lemon juice
- 1 teaspoon ground cumin
- 1 teaspoon spicy Hungarian paprika
- 1 teaspoon red chili powder
- Salt and ground black pepper, as required 1 whole trout, cleaned

Instructions:

- Preheat the Outdoor Gas Griddle to medium-high heat.
- In a bowl, blend together oil and remaining ingredients except for trout.
- With a knife, make deep cuts in each side of trout.
- Rub the trout with spice mixture generously.
- Arrange the trout in a dish and refrigerate to marinate for at least 1 hour.
- Grease the griddle.
- Place the trout onto the griddle and cook for about 5 minutes from each side.
- Serve hot.

Simple Haddock

(Preparation time: 10 minutes | **Cooking time:** 5 minutes| **Servings:** 4)

Ingredients:

- 4 (4-ounce) haddock fillets
- Salt and ground black pepper, as required

Instructions:

- Preheat the Outdoor Gas Griddle to medium heat.
- Grease the griddle.
- Sprinkle the haddock fillets generously with salt and black pepper.
- Place the haddock fillets onto the griddle and cook for about 4-5
- minutes, flipping once.
- Serve hot.

Tuna Skewers

(Preparation time: 15 minutes | **Cooking time:** 5 minutes| **Servings:** 2)

Ingredients:

- ¾ ounce sesame oil
- 8 ounces fresh tuna steak, cut into 1-inch cubes
- 3-4 ounces teriyaki sauce

- ½ tablespoons ginger garlic paste
- 1 tablespoon fresh lemon juice

Instructions:

- Preheat the Outdoor Gas Griddle to high heat.
- Mix together all the ingredients except tuna steak in a bowl.
- Marinate tuna in this mixture for about 1 hour.
- Thread the tuna cubes onto the skewers.
- Place the skewers of tuna onto the griddle and cook for about 4-5
- minutes, flipping occasionally.
- Serve hot.

Crusted Scallops

(**Preparation time:** 15 minutes | **Cooking time:** 10 minutes| **Servings:** 4)

Ingredients:

- ½ cup olive oil
- ¼ cup Parmesan cheese, shredded
- ½ cup fine Italian breadcrumbs
- ½ teaspoon garlic salt
- 1 teaspoon dried parsley, crushed ½ teaspoon ground black pepper
- 16 large sea scallops

Instructions:

- In a shallow dish, place oil.
- In another shallow dish, mix together cheese, bread crumbs, garlic salt, parsley and black pepper.
- Dip the scallops in oil and then roll in cheese mixture evenly.
- Arrange the scallops onto a large plate in a single layer.
- Refrigerate for at least 30 minutes.
- Preheat the Outdoor Gas Griddle to medium-high heat.
- Grease the griddle.
- Coat the scallops evenly with oil.
- Place the scallops onto the griddle and cook for about 5 minutes per side or until desired doneness.

Shrimp Kabobs

(**Preparation time:** 15 minutes | **Cooking time:** 6 minutes| **Servings:** 3)

Ingredients:

- 2 garlic cloves, minced
- 3 tablespoons fresh lemon juice
- 1 tablespoon Dijon mustard
- 1 tablespoon agave nectar
- 1 tablespoon low-sodium soy sauce
- 2 teaspoons curry paste
- 1 pound medium shrimp, peeled and deveined

Instructions:

- In a bowl, add garlic and remaining ingredients, except for shrimp, and mix until well combined.
- Add shrimp and coat with marinade generously.
- Cover the bowl of shrimp mixture and refrigerate to marinate for about 1 hour.
- Preheat the Outdoor Gas Griddle to high heat.
- Thread the shrimp onto pre-soaked wooden skewers.
- Grease the griddle.
- Arrange the skewers of shrimp onto the griddle and cook for about 3
- minutes per side, brushing with marinade occasionally.
- Serve hot.

Appetizer Recipes

Scallops Orange Skewers

(**Preparation time:** 10 minutes | **Cooking time:** 10 minutes | **Servings:** 2)

Ingredients:

- 12 scallops
- 1 tablespoon ginger, grated
- 1 orange, cut into pieces
- 1 tablespoon honey
- Pepper
- Salt

Instructions:

- In a small bowl, mix honey, ginger, pepper, and salt.
- Thread scallops and orange pieces onto the skewers and brush with honey mixture.
- Preheat the Griddle to medium heat.
- Place skewers on a hot griddle top and cooks for 2-3 minutes on each side.
- Servings and enjoy.

Tasty Bread Pizza

(**Preparation time:** 10 minutes | **Cooking time:** 10 minutes | **Servings:** 4)

Ingredients:

- 4 bread slices
- For toppings:
- 10 olives, sliced
- 1 small tomato, cubed
- 1/2 cup bell pepper, cubed
- 1 onion, cubed
- 1/4 teaspoons red chili flakes
- 1/2 teaspoons oregano
- 1/2 cup mozzarella cheese, grated
- 2 tablespoons pizza sauce

Instructions:

- Spread pizza sauce on bread slices. Top with tomatoes, olives, bell pepper, and onion.
- Sprinkle with chili flakes, oregano, and cheese.
- Preheat the Griddle to medium heat.
- Place bread slices on hot griddle top and cover and cook until cheese is melted.
- Servings and enjoy.

Corn Cakes

(Preparation time: 10 minutes | **Cooking time:** 10 minutes| **Servings:** 10)

Ingredients:

- 4 eggs
- 2 cups corn
- 1/2 teaspoons pepper
- 1/2 cup cornmeal
- 1/2 cup flour
- 1/2 cup cheddar cheese, shredded
- 2/3 cup green onions, sliced
- 1 jalapeno, chopped
- 1/2 teaspoons kosher salt

Instructions:

- Add corn into the food processor and process until roughly chopped.
- Add corn and remaining ingredients into the mixing bowl and mix until well combined.
- Preheat the Griddle to high heat.
- Spray griddle top with cooking spray.
- Make patties from mixture and place on hot griddle top and cook until lightly golden brown from both sides.
- Servings and enjoy.

Tuna Patties

(Preparation time: 10 minutes | **Cooking time:** 10 minutes| **Servings:** 4)

Ingredients:

- 1 egg
- 10 oz can tuna, drained
- 25 crackers, crushed

- 1/4 teaspoons pepper
- 2 teaspoons Dijon mustard
- 1 tablespoon mayonnaise
- 1/4 cup onion, chopped
- 1/4 teaspoons salt

Instructions:

- Mix all the ingredients.
- Preheat the Griddle to high heat.
- Spray griddle top with cooking spray.
- Make patties from mixture, place on hot griddle top, and cook until lightly golden brown from both sides.

Quick Cheese Toast

(**Preparation time:** 10 minutes | **Cooking time:** 8 minutes| **Servings:** 4)

Ingredients:

- 8 bread slices
- 4 garlic cloves, minced
- 2 green chili, chopped
- 1 cup mozzarella cheese, shredded
- 1 cup bell pepper, chopped
- Pepper
- Salt

Instructions:

- Mix bell pepper, green chili, and garlic and spread evenly over bread slices. Top with cheese, pepper, and salt.
- Preheat the Griddle to medium heat.
- Spray griddle top with cooking spray.
- Place bread slices on hot griddle top cover and cook until cheese melts.
- Servings and enjoy.

Tomato Avocado Bruschetta

(**Preparation time:** 10 minutes | **Cooking time:** 10 minutes| **Servings:** 6)

Ingredients:

- 6 bread slices
- 2 tablespoons olive oil

- For topping:
- 1 tomato, chopped
- 1 garlic clove, minced
- 1 cucumber, diced
- 1 avocado, peel & dice
- 1/4 teaspoon sea salt

Instructions:

- Preheat the Griddle to high heat.
- Brush bread with oil and place on hot griddle top and cook until lightly golden brown from both sides.
- Add all topping ingredients and mix well.
- Spoon topping mixture over bread slices.
- Servings and enjoy.

Spicy Chicken Burger Patties

(Preparation time: 10 minutes | **Cooking time:** 12 minutes| **Servings:** 6)

Ingredients:

- 1 lb ground chicken
- 1 teaspoon chili powder
- 1 teaspoon cayenne powder
- 1 tablespoon honey
- 1/4 cup almond flour
- 1/4 teaspoons pepper
- 2 teaspoons dried parsley
- 1 teaspoon paprika
- 1/4 teaspoons salt

Instructions:

- Mix all the ingredients.
- Preheat the Griddle to high heat.
- Spray griddle top with cooking spray.
- Make patties from mixture and place on hot griddle top and cook for 4-6
- minutes on each side.
- Servings and enjoy.

Walnuts Bowls

(Preparation time: 5 minutes | **Cooking time:** 3 minutes| **Servings:** 4)

Ingredients:

- 2 cups walnuts
- ½ teaspoon hot paprika
- 1 tablespoon olive oil
- 1 teaspoon red pepper flakes, crushed
- 1 tablespoon lime juice
- 1 tablespoon capers, drained
- 1 tablespoon chives, chopped

Instructions:

- Mix nuts with paprika and other ingredients, place on Griddle, and roast for 3 minutes.
- Divide the mix into bowls and serve as a snack.

Radish with Herb Cheese

(**Preparation time:** 15 minutes | **Cooking time:** 10 minutes | **Servings:** 3)

Ingredients:

- 10 oz goat cheese
- 4 oz cream cheese
- ¼ cup red bell pepper, minced
- 3 tablespoons pesto
- 3 teaspoons lemon juice
- 2 tablespoons parsley
- 2 clove garlic
- 9 large radishes, sliced.

Instructions:

- Place the radish slices onto the Griddle and cook for 8/10 minutes.
- In a bowl, mix the remaining listed ingredients. Once the radish is cooked, arrange the slices on a serving platter and pipe the cheese mixture on each slice. Serve as a snack.

Healthy Broccoli

(**Preparation time:** 10 minutes | **Cooking time:** 6 minutes | **Servings:** 6)

Ingredients:

- 4 cups broccoli florets

- 1 1/2 teaspoons garlic, minced
- 1 1/2 teaspoons Italian seasoning
- 1 tablespoon lemon juice
- 4 tablespoons olive oil
- 1/4 teaspoons pepper
- 1 1/4 teaspoons kosher salt

Instructions:

- Add broccoli and remaining ingredients into the bowl and mix well.
- Cover and place in the refrigerator for 1 hour.
- Preheat the Griddle to high heat.
- Spray griddle top with cooking spray.
- Place broccoli florets on a hot griddle top and cook for 3 minutes on each side.
- Servings and enjoy.

Easy Pineapple Slices

(Preparation time: 10 minutes | **Cooking time:** 12 minutes| **Servings:** 4)

Ingredients:

- 4 pineapple slices
- 1 tablespoon butter, melted
- 1/4 teaspoons chili powder
- Salt

Instructions:

- Preheat the Griddle to high heat.
- Brush pineapple slices with butter, chili powder, and salt.
- Place pineapple slices on a hot griddle top and cook for 5-6 minutes on each side.
- Servings and enjoy.

Tortilla Pizza

(Preparation time: 10 minutes | **Cooking time:** 5 minutes| **Servings:** 1)

Ingredients:

- 1 tortilla
- For topping:
- 1/4 teaspoons red chili flakes
- 1/4 teaspoons dried oregano
- 1/2 teaspoons garlic, minced

- 2 teaspoons onion, chopped
- 1/4 cup tomatoes, chopped
- 3 tablespoons mozzarella cheese, shredded
- Pepper
- Salt

Instructions:

- Add tomatoes, onion, garlic, oregano, chili flakes, cheese, pepper, and salt to a tortilla.
- Preheat the Griddle to high heat.
- Spray griddle top with cooking spray.
- Place tortilla on hot griddle top cover and cook until cheese melts.
- Servings and enjoy.

Chickpea Burger Patties

(**Preparation time:** 10 minutes | **Cooking time:** 12 minutes | **Servings:** 6)

Ingredients:

- 3 eggs
- 1 3/4 cups can chickpeas, drained
- 2 cups cauliflower florets
- 1/2 teaspoons onion powder
- 1 teaspoon garlic powder
- 2 tablespoons parsley, chopped
- 1/2 cup onion, chopped
- Pepper
- Salt

Instructions:

- Add cauliflower florets and chickpeas into the food processor and process until finely chopped.
- Add remaining ingredients and process until just combined.
- Preheat the Griddle to medium heat.
- Make patties from mixture and place on hot griddle top and cook until lightly browned from both sides.
- Servings and enjoy

Veggie Patties

(**Preparation time:** 10 minutes | **Cooking time:** 10 minutes | **Servings:** 6)

Ingredients:

- 2 eggs
- 2 tablespoons parsley, chopped
- 1/2 cup onion, chopped
- 1 cup potatoes, shredded
- 1 cup zucchini, shredded
- 1 cup carrots, shredded
- 1 cup breadcrumbs
- Pepper
- Salt

Instructions:

- Mix all the ingredients.
- 2. Preheat the Griddle to high heat.
- 3. Spray griddle top with cooking spray.
- 4. Make patties from mixture and place on hot griddle top and cook until lightly golden brown from both sides.
- 5. Servings and enjoy.

Dessert Recipes

Honey Fruit on the Griddle

(Preparation time: 5 minutes | **Cooking time:** 10 minutes| **Servings:** 4)

Ingredients:

- 2 plums, peaches apricots, etc. (choose seasonally) 3 tablespoons Sugar, turbinate
- ¼ cup of Honey
- Gelato, as desired

Instructions:

- Preheat the Griddle to 450°F with closed lid, slice each fruit in halves and remove pits. Brush with honey. Sprinkle with some sugar.
- Griddle on the grate until you see that there are griddle marks. Set aside, serve each with a scoop of gelato. Enjoy.

Yummy Apple Pie on the Griddle with Cinnamon

(Preparation time: 15 minutes | **Cooking time:** 30 minutes| **Servings:** 6)

Ingredients:

- ¼ cup of Sugar
- 4 Apples, sliced
- 1 tablespoon of Cornstarch
- 1 teaspoon Cinnamon, ground
- 1 Pie Crust, refrigerated, soften in according to the directions on the box
- ½ cup of Peach preserves

Instructions:

- Preheat the Griddle to 375°F with closed lid, in a bowl combine the cinnamon, cornstarch, sugar, and apples. Set aside. Place the piecrust in a pie
- pan. Spread the preserves and then place the apples. Fold the crust slightly.
- Place a pan on the Griddle (upside - down) so that you don't brill/bake the pie directly on the heat, cook 30 - 40 minutes. Once done, set aside to rest.
- Serve and enjoy

Simple Coconut

(Preparation time: 15 minutes | **Cooking time:** 30 minutes| **Servings:** 6)

Ingredients:

- 4 eggs
- 1 cup Cane Sugar
- ¾ cup of Coconut oil
- 4 ounces chocolate, chopped
- ½ teaspoon of Sea salt
- ¼ cup cocoa powder, unsweetened
- ½ cup flour
- 4 ounces Chocolate chips
- 1 teaspoon of Vanilla

Instructions:

- Preheat the Griddle to 350°F with closed lid, take a baking pan (9x9), grease it and line a parchment paper.
- In a bowl combine the salt, cocoa powder and flour. Stir and set aside, in the microwave or double boiler melt the coconut oil and chopped chocolate.
- Let it cool a bit, add the vanilla, eggs, and sugar. Whisk to combine.
- Add into the flour, and add chocolate chips. Add the mixture into a pan, put the pan on the grate. Bake for 20 minutes. If you want dryer brownies to bake for 5 - 10 minutes more. Let them cool before cutting. Cut the brownies into squares and serve.

Vanilla Bacon Chocolate Chip Cookies

(**Preparation time:** 30 minutes | **Cooking time:** 30 minutes| **Servings:** 6)

Ingredients:

- 8 slices cooked and crumbled bacon
- 2 ½ teaspoons apple cider vinegar
- 1 teaspoon vanilla
- 2 cups semisweet chocolate chips
- 2 room temp eggs
- 1 ½ teaspoon baking soda
- 1 cup granulated sugar
- ½ teaspoon salt
- 2 ¾ cup all-purpose flour
- 1 cup light brown sugar
- 1 ½ stick softened butter

Instructions:

- Mix salt, baking soda and flour, cream the sugar and the butter together.

- Lower the speed. Add in the eggs, vinegar, and vanilla. Put it on low fire, slowly add in the flour mixture, bacon pieces, and chocolate chips.
- Preheat your Griddle, with your lid closed, until it reaches 375°F, put a parchment paper on a baking sheet you are using and drop a teaspoonful of cookie batter on the baking sheet. Let them cook on the Griddle, covered, for approximately 12 minutes or until they are browned.

Walnut Chocolate Chip Cookies

(**Preparation time:** 30 minutes | **Cooking time:** 30 minutes| **Servings:** 8)

Ingredients:

- 1 ½ cup chopped walnuts
- 1 teaspoon vanilla
- 2 cup chocolate chips
- 1 teaspoon baking soda
- 2 ½ cup plain flour
- ½ teaspoon salt
- 1 ½ stick softened butter
- 2 eggs
- 1 cup brown sugar
- ½ cup sugar

Instructions:

- Preheat your Griddle, with your lid closed, until it reaches 350°F, mix the baking soda, salt, and flour. Cream the brown sugar, sugar, and butter. Mix in the vanilla and eggs until it comes together.
- Slowly add in the flour while continuing to beat. When all flour has been incorporated, add the chocolate chips and walnuts. Using a spoon, fold into batter.
- Place an aluminum foil onto Griddle. In an aluminum foil, drop spoonful of
- dough and bake for 17 minutes.

Cinnamon Apple Cobbler

(**Preparation time:** 30 minutes | **Cooking time:** 70 minutes| **Servings:** 8)

Ingredients:

- 8 Granny Smith apples
- 1 cup sugar
- 1 stick melted butter
- 1 teaspoon cinnamon

- Pinch salt
- ½ cup brown sugar
- 2 eggs
- 2 teaspoons baking powder
- 2 cup plain flour
- 1 ½ cup sugar

Instructions:

- Peel and quarter apples, place into a bowl. Add in the cinnamon and one c.
- sugar. Stir well to coat and let it set for one hour. Preheat your Griddle, with your lid closed, until it reaches 350.
- In a large bowl add the salt, baking powder, eggs, brown sugar, sugar, and flour. Mix until it forms crumbles.
- Place apples into rack Add the crumble mixture on top and drizzle with melted butter, place on the Griddle and cook for 50 minutes.

Bananas in Caramel Sauce

(**Preparation time:** 15 minutes | **Cooking time:** 15 minutes| **Servings:** 4)

Ingredients:

- ⅓ cup chopped pecans
- ½ cup sweetened condensed milk
- 4 slightly green bananas
- ½ cup brown sugar
- 2 tablespoons corn syrup
- ½ cup butter

Instructions:

- Preheat your Griddle, with the lid closed, until it reaches 350°F, place the milk, corn syrup, butter, and brown sugar into a heavy saucepan and bring to boil. For five minutes simmer the mixture in low heat. Stir frequently.
- Place the bananas with their peels on, on the Griddle and let them griddle for five minutes. Flip and cook for five minutes more. Peels will be dark and might split.
- Place on serving platter. Cut the ends off the bananas and split peel down the middle. Take the peel off the bananas and spoon caramel on top. Sprinkle with pecans.

Ice Cream Bread with Chocolate Chips

(**Preparation time:** 10 minutes | **Cooking time:** 60 minutes| **Servings:** 6)

Ingredients:

- 1 ½ quart full-fat butter pecan ice cream, softened 1 teaspoon salt
- 2 cups semisweet chocolate chips
- 1 cup sugar
- 1 stick melted butter
- Butter, for greasing
- 4 cups self-rising flour

Instructions:

- Preheat your Griddle, with your lid closed, until it reaches 350°F, mix together the salt, sugar, flour, and ice cream with an electric mixer set to medium for two minutes.
- As the mixer is still running, add in the chocolate chips, beating until everything is blended, spray a pan with cooking spray. If you choose to use a pan that is solid, the center will take too long to cook.
- That's why a tube or Bundt pan works best. Add the batter to your Prepared pan, set the cake on the Griddle, cover, and smoke for 50 minutes to an hour.
- A toothpick should come out clean. 4.Take the pan off of the Griddle. For 10
- minutes cool the bread. Remove carefully the bread from the pan and then drizzle it with some melted butter

Sugar Pumpkin Seeds with Cinnamon

(**Preparation time:** 15 minutes | **Cooking time:** 30 minutes| **Servings:** 8)

Ingredients:

- 2 tablespoons sugar
- Seeds from a pumpkin
- 1 teaspoon cinnamon
- 2 tablespoons melted butter

Instructions:

- Preheat your Griddle, with your lid closed, until it reaches 350°F, clean the seeds and toss them in the melted butter. Add them to the sugar and cinnamon. Spread them on a sheet, place on the Griddle, and smoke for 25 minutes. Serve.

Mint Julep Peaches

(**Preparation time:** 10 minutes | **Cooking time:** 10 minutes| **Servings:** 4)

Ingredients:

- ½ cup of shortening
- 2 cups of packed dark brown sugar
- 4 ripe peaches
- 2 cups of vanilla bean ice cream
- ½ cup of Kentucky Bourbon
- 4 stems separated sprigs mint

Instructions:

- Preheat your griddle at medium-high temperature, in a small-sized saucepan on the Griddle, combine the bourbon, brown sugar, & mint stems. Allow 5 min for the sauce to reduce.
- Remove the stones from the peaches and cut them in half, the shortening should be applied uniformly to the flesh. Peaches should be cooked for around 2 min with the shortening side down and tented using foil.
- Rotate them at 180 degrees and cook for another 2 min, covered, drizzle glaze over the peaches, flesh side up. Serve with ice cream & fresh mint leaves on top.

Watermelon with yogurt

(**Preparation time:** 10 minutes | **Cooking time:** 10 minutes| **Servings:** 6)

Ingredients:

- 1 tablespoon of white wine vinegar
- 1 cup of plain Greek yogurt
- 1/4 cup of small mint leaves
- 2 tablespoons of lemon juice
- 1 tablespoon of e.v. olive oil, plus more for the drizzling Sea salt for seasoning
- 1 teaspoon of coarsely chopped thyme
- Honey, for drizzling
- Twelve 3-inch-long triangles of the seedless red watermelon, around 1-
- inch thick

Instructions:

- Preheat your griddle at a high temperature, in a small-sized mixing dish, combine the yogurt, thyme, lemon juice, vinegar, & 1 tablespoon of olive oil.
- Season the watermelon triangles using salt and drizzle with olive oil, cook for around 1 minute on each side till charred; transfer to plates.
- Season the watermelon using black pepper and a dollop of yogurt sauce, to serve, garnish with mint and a drizzle of honey.

Pound Cake with Sour Cherry Syrup

(Preparation time: 10 minutes | **Cooking time:** 20 minutes| **Servings:** 12)

Ingredients:

- 4 tablespoons of sea salt
- ½ teaspoon of fresh lemon juice
- 1 ⅓ lbs. of fresh cherries
- 2 tablespoons of brown sugar, packed
- ¾ cup of sugar
- 1 cup of sour cream
- 1 pound of cake, cut into 8 slices

Instructions:

- Preheat your griddle at medium temperature, in a medium-sized saucepan on the Griddle, bring the cherries, sugar, 1/4 cup of water, & salt to the boil. Cook, stirring periodically, for around 10 min, till a syrup develops.
- Allow cooling.
- In a small-sized mixing bowl, combine sour cream, brown sugar, & lemon, juice; chill till ready to serve, cook for around 1 minute on each side of the pound cake on the Griddle. Place a dollop of sour cream mixture & 1/3 cup cherry syrup on each slice of pound cake and serve.

Seasonal Fruit with Gelato

(Preparation time: 5 minutes | **Cooking time:** 10 minutes| **Servings:** 2)

Ingredients:

- 1/4 cup of honey
- 3 tablespoons of turbinado sugar
- Your preferred gelato for serving
- 2 whole seasonal fruits: apricots, plums or peaches

Instructions:

- Before cooking, preheat your griddle at 400°F and cover for around 15 min, remove the pit from each apple before slicing it in half. Sugar should be placed on top, and honey should be sprayed on the cutting side.
- Cook the fruit with the trim side down on the Griddle till charred.
- Remove the fruits from the Griddle and serve with a scoop of gelato right away. If desired, drizzle with honey. Enjoy!

Griddled Strawberry e Pineapple

(**Preparation time:** 15 minutes | **Cooking time:** 10 minutes | **Servings:** 8)

Ingredients:

- 2 cups pineapple, cut into 1-inch chunks
- 2 cups fresh strawberries, hulled
- Olive oil cooking spray
- 2 tablespoons maple syrup

Instructions:

- Preheat the Outdoor Gas Griddle to medium-low heat.
- Thread the fruit pieces onto the pre-soaked wooden skewer.
- Spray the skewers with cooking spray and then drizzle with maple syrup.
- Grease the Griddle lightly.
- Arrange the skewers of fruit onto the Griddle and cook for about 10
- minutes, flipping occasionally.
- Serve immediately.

French Toast Skewers

(**Preparation time:** 15 minutes | **Cooking time:** 10 minutes | **Servings:** 6)

Ingredients:

- 3 eggs
- ½ cup milk
- 1 teaspoon vanilla extract
- ½ teaspoon ground cinnamon
- 5 cups crusty bread cubes
- 2-3 tablespoons maple syrup

Instructions:

- Preheat the Outdoor Gas Griddle to medium-low heat.
- Whisk together the eggs, milk, vanilla extract and cinnamon in a bowl.
- Coat the bread cubes evenly with egg mixture.
- Thread the bread cubes onto pre-soaked wooden skewers.
- Grease the Griddle.
- Arrange the skewers of bread cubes onto the Griddle and cook for about 4-5 minutes per side.
- Serve with a drizzling of maple syrup.

Cream Cheese e Jam Stuffed

(Preparation time: 10 minutes | **Cooking time:** 6 minutes| **Servings:** 4)

Ingredients:

- 8 bread slices
- ½ cup cream cheese, softened
- 4 tablespoons raspberry jam
- 4 eggs
- 4 tablespoons butter

Instructions:

- Preheat the Outdoor Gas Griddle to medium heat.
- Arrange 2 bread slices onto a plate.
- Spread 2 tablespoons of cream cheese onto 1 bread slice.
- Spread 1 tablespoon of jam onto the other slice.
- Place the jam side-down over the cream cheese.
- Repeat with the remaining slices, cream cheese and jam.
- In a shallow dish, whisk the eggs.
- Dip both sides of sandwiches into beaten eggs evenly.
- Grease the Griddle lightly.
- Place the sandwiches onto the Griddle and cook for about 3 minutes per side or until golden brown.
- Cut 2 halves of each sandwich and serve warm

Chocolate-Stuffed French Toast

(Preparation time: 10 minutes | **Cooking time:** 6 minutes| **Servings:** 12)

Ingredients:

- 1 cup whole milk
- 3 large eggs
- 1 teaspoon sugar
- 1 teaspoon vanilla extract
- Pinch of salt
- 12 bread slices
- 3 (1½-ounce) chocolate bars, halved

Instructions:

- Preheat the Outdoor Gas Griddle to medium heat.
- Whisk together the milk, eggs, sugar, vanilla extract and salt.
- Place 1 chocolate piece over 6 bread slices.
- Cover with remaining bread slices.
- Dip both sides of sandwiches into beaten eggs evenly.
- Grease the Griddle lightly.
- Place the sandwiches onto the Griddle and cook for about 3-4 minutes per side or until golden brown.
- Cut 2 halves of each sandwich and serve warm.

Chocolate Cherry Griddled

(**Preparation time:** 10 minutes | **Cooking time:** 8 minutes| **Servings:** 12)

Ingredients:

- 12 (½-inch-thick) bread slices
- 3 tablespoons cherry preserves
- 2 (4-ounce) bittersweet chocolate bars, cut each into thirds
- 1/3 cup unsalted butter, melted

Instructions:

- Preheat the Outdoor Gas Griddle to medium-low heat.
- Arrange the bread slices onto a smooth surface.
- Spread the cherry preserves onto 6 bread slices.
- Top each slice with 1 piece of chocolate.
- Cover with the remaining bread slices.
- Brush both sides of each sandwich the melted butter.
- Place the sandwiches onto the Griddle and cook for about 2-4 minutes per side.
- Cut 2 halves of each sandwich and serve warm.

Chocolate Marshmallow Waffle

(**Preparation time:** 10 minutes | **Cooking time:** 10 minutes| **Servings:** 8)

Ingredients:

- 8 frozen waffles
- 1 cup miniature marshmallows
- 1 cup semi-sweet chocolate chips

Instructions:

- Preheat the Outdoor Gas Griddle to medium heat.
- Arrange 4 (12-inch square) greased pieces of a double thickness of heavy-duty foil onto a smooth surface.
- Place one waffle onto 1 piece of foil and top with marshmallows and chocolate chips.
- Cover with one of the remaining waffles.
- Fold foil around the sandwich and seal tightly.
- Repeat with remaining waffles, marshmallows and chocolate chips.
- Arrange the foil packets onto the Griddle and cover with a cooking dome.
- Cook for about 8-10 minutes or until chocolate is melted, flipping once halfway through.
- Cut each waffle sandwich in half and serve warm.

Chocolate S'mores

(**Preparation time:** 10 minutes | **Cooking time:** 5 minutes | **Servings:** 4)

Ingredients:

- 8 individual graham crackers
- 1 ounce semisweet chocolate bar, broken into 4 pieces 4 large marshmallows

Instructions:

- Preheat half of the Outdoor Gas Griddle to medium-high heat.
- Preheat the remaining half of Griddle to low heat.
- Grease the Griddle lightly.
- Place graham cracker halves onto the low heated side of Griddle.
- Top 4 crackers with chocolate and remaining 4 marshmallows.
- With the cooking dome, cover the crackers and cook for about 3-5
- minutes.
- Place marshmallow crackers over chocolate crackers and serve.

Cinnamon Roll Pancakes

(**Preparation time:** 15 minutes | **Cooking time:** 5 minutes | **Servings:** 6)

Ingredients:

- 8 1 cup biscuit baking mix
- 1 egg
- ½ cup milk
- 4 tablespoons butter, melted

- 1/3 cup brown sugar
- 1½ teaspoons ground cinnamon
- 2 ounces cream cheese, softened
- 4 tablespoons butter, softened
- ¾ cup powdered sugar, divided
- ½ teaspoon vanilla extract

Instructions:

- Preheat the Outdoor Gas Griddle to medium heat.
- Whisk together the biscuit baking mix, egg and milk in a mixing bowl. Set aside.
- For filling: whisk together the melted butter, brown sugar and cinnamon into a bowl.
- Whisk together the cream cheese and softened butter in a bowl until smooth.
- Place the butter mixture in a bag with a tiny hole. Set aside.
- For glaze: Whisk together the cream cheese and softened butter in a bowl until creamy and smooth.
- In the bowl of cream cheese, add in the powdered sugar and vanilla extract and whisk until smooth. Set aside.
- Grease the Griddle generously.
- Place about ¼ cup of the mixture onto the Griddle and spread in an even layer.
- Repeat with the remaining mixture.
- Carefully squeeze the piping bag of filling in a spiral onto the top of each pancake.
- Cook each pancake for about 2-3 minutes or until golden brown.
- Carefully flip the pancakes and cook for about 2 minutes or until golden brown.
- Transfer the pancakes onto a platter.
- Drizzle with glaze and serve.

Vanilla Cupcakes

(**Preparation time:** 20 minutes | **Cooking time:** 10 minutes | **Servings:** 24)

Ingredients:

Cupcakes

- 1 (15¼-ounce) package yellow cake mix
- 3 large eggs
- 1 cup water
- 1/3 cup vegetable oil

Frosting

- 2 cup unsalted butter, softened

- 9 cups powdered sugar
- 2 tablespoon pure vanilla extract
- 8-10 tablespoons heavy cream

Instructions:

- Preheat the Outdoor Gas Griddle to low heat.
- Line 4 (6-cup) metal cupcake pans with paper liners.

For cupcakes

- Add cake mix, eggs, water and oil in a bowl and mix until just combined.
- Place the mixture into the prepared pans about 2/3 of the full.
- Place the cupcake pans onto the Griddle and cover with a cooking dome.
- Cook for about 9-10 minutes or until a wooden skewer inserted in the center of the cupcake comes out clean.
- Remove the cupcake pans from Griddle and place onto 2 wire racks to cool for about 10 minutes.
- Carefully turn the cupcakes onto the wire racks to cool completely before frosting.

For frosting

- In a bowl, add the softened butter and with an electric mixer, beat on medium speed until soft and creamy.
- Add in the powdered sugar in little batches and beat on medium speed until well combined.
- Add the vanilla extract and beat until well combined.
- Slowly add in the heavy cream, 1 tablespoon at a time and beat until smooth.
- Spread frosting over cooled cupcakes and serve.

Griddle Fruit with Cream

(**Preparation time:** 15 minutes | **Cooking time:** 10 minutes| **Servings:** 6)

Ingredients:

- 2 halved apricots
- 1 halved nectarine
- 2 halved peaches
- ¼ cup of blueberries
- ½ cup of raspberries
- 2 tbsp of honey
- 1 orange, the peel
- 2 cups of cream

- ½ cup of balsamic vinegar

Instructions:

- Preheat the Griddle to 400°F with a closed lid.
- Griddle the peaches, nectarines and apricots for 4 minutes on each side.
- Place a pan over the stove and turn on medium heat. Add 2 tbsp of honey, vinegar, and orange peel. Simmer until medium thick.
- In the meantime, add honey and cream to a bowl. Whip until it reaches a soft form.
- Place the fruits on a serving plate. Sprinkle with berries. Drizzle with balsamic reduction. Servings with cream and enjoy!

Apple Pie on the Griddle

(**Preparation time:** 15 minutes | **Cooking time:** 30 minutes| **Servings:** 6)

Ingredients:

- ¼ cup of sugar
- 4 apples, sliced
- 1 tbsp of cornstarch
- 1 tsp cinnamon, ground
- 1 pie crust, refrigerated, soften according to the directions on the box ½ cup of peach preserving

Instructions:

- Preheat the Griddle to 375°F with a closed lid.
- In a bowl combine the cinnamon, cornstarch, sugar, and apples. Set aside.
- Place the pie crust in a pie pan. Spread the preserving and then place the apples. Fold the crust slightly.
- Place a pan on the Griddle (upside-down) so that you don't brill/bake the pie directly on the heat.
- Cook 30 - 40 minutes. Once done, set aside to rest. Servings and enjoy

Griddle Layered Cake

(**Preparation time:** 10 minutes | **Cooking time:** 20 minutes| **Servings:** 6)

Ingredients:

- 2 2 x lb. cake
- 3 cups of whipped cream
- ¼ cup melted butter
- 1 cup of blueberries
- 1 cup of raspberries

- 1 cup sliced strawberries

Instructions:

- Preheat the Griddle to high with a closed lid.
- Slice the cake loaf (¾ inch), about 10 per loaf. Brush both sides with butter.
- Griddle for 7 minutes on each side. Set aside.
- Once cooled completely start layering your cake. Place cake, berries then cream.
- Sprinkle with berries and Servings.

Conclusions

The Outdoor Gas Griddle is a fantastic addition to your outdoor kitchens since it will enable you to prepare food for larger numbers and allow you to enjoy large outdoor meals. You may create a wide range of different meals using it as both a flat-top and a griddle. The appliance includes two built-in side burners with high BTU output that make it simple to boil water, cook bacon, and prepare other things. The overall durability and use of strong gauge stainless steel assure that, with correct maintenance, you will always have a heating surface.

Additional Features

The Outdoor Gas Griddle has adjustable heat settings that will be able to regulate the temperature of the surface, which gives you many options to choose from. The unit also has one side burner that offers high BTUs and two built-in side burners located on either side of the unit. These side burners are unique since you can cook food on the top of the Griddle, cook food directly over or to one side of it, or place any type of cooking utensil directly into them.

Energy Efficiency/Environmental Impact

Since the Outside Gas Griddle is intended for outdoor usage, it may rust over time if not properly preserved. But because the Griddle is built of high gauge stainless steel, it will be strong and able to resist many years of rigorous use. The unit is highly durable and can support over 200 pounds without bending because the legs are made of solid stainless steel. This will enable you to use the Griddle properly and ensure that it doesn't tip over and perhaps harm other household appliances or itself.

The Outdoor Gas Griddle is propane-operated, so you will be using gas when cooking with this unit. Propane should only be used outdoors because if there is any leak, then you could end up with an explosion or fire hazard in your home.

Made in the USA
Las Vegas, NV
11 December 2022